The New England
BUTT'RY SHELF COOKBOOK
Receipts for
Very Special Occasions

The New England
BUTT'RY SHELF
COOKBOOK

Receipts for
Very Special Occasions

MARY MASON CAMPBELL

ILLUSTRATED BY

TASHA TUDOR

THE WORLD PUBLISHING COMPANY

CLEVELAND · NEW YORK

Published by The World Publishing Company
2231 West 110th Street, Cleveland, Ohio 44102
Published simultaneously in Canada by Nelson, Foster & Scott Ltd.

THIRD PRINTING *1969*

Library of Congress Catalog Card Number 67–22907

A SUGAR COOKY
FOR
Douglas
AND THE
Mason Girls

Contents

COLOR ILLUSTRATIONS

The Buttery Book

CITY people used to have pantries. The country counterpart of the pantry was called a "butt'ry." In occasional hidden corners of New England, this country room may still be found in use, but only the most old-fashioned houses, loved and lived in by the most old-fashioned kind of people, have a "butt'ry" these days.

The butt'ry (properly spelled *buttery*, of course) is a small room with a smell of good things to eat and a look of delicious plenty. It is located next to the kitchen in the cool corner of the house. Its window is shaded in summer by a crab-apple tree. We can watch a robin and her mate busily raising their family in the nest tucked between branches. We can reach out the window with a long-nosed watering can to give a drink to the fuchsia and begonia plants trailing their flowery stems in the dappled shade of the leaves. Through the window, we watch the lilacs and the old-fashioned roses come into bloom, and enjoy a view of the perennial border against its background of gray stone wall as its colors and patterns change from the daffodils of early spring to the last flowering chrysanthemum of the autumn.

In the winter, the bird feeder is easy to reach from the window, and who minds if we dip overmuch into the sugar bucket when whipping up a cake if we are diverted by the arrival of a cardinal or rose-breasted grosbeak on the windowsill? In the winter now the butt'ry is warm and cheerful, though in years gone by it was often bitter cold and the New England house-wife who never dreamed of such a thing as an electric freezer kept her store of frozen pies and muffins and cookies handy to the kitchen on a shelf of the butt'ry.

Sheathed in warm-colored pine boards, the walls of the butt'ry are lined with hand-planed shelves, sturdy enough to bear the weight of jars, crocks, platters, and plates filled with the richness of country cooking. On the floor under the shelves are the bins of flour and the wooden bucket of sugar. Here are the stacks of milk pans and pails, the churns, the breadboard in place against the wall, to be pulled out often and placed on the wide shelf in front of the window, floured for rolling out cookies, pie and biscuit dough, or kneading bread, then dusted off and replaced in its niche. A big basket of apples fits into the corner; a pan of potatoes brought up from the cellar is next to the apples. Several battered lard pails and a half-dozen old Shaker-made wooden blueberry boxes await July blueberry-picking time.

Here too is kept the crock of tutti-frutti, which is as much a part of the butt'ry equipment as anything else you can see there. It holds two gallons of rich fruit sauce for ladling generously onto a plate of vanilla ice cream or a slice of pound or sponge cake, and I've known many a time when a finger was surreptitiously dipped in and popped into an appreciative mouth for elegant tasting. The jar is always empty by the time the first fresh straw-berries are brought in from the garden, washed clean then, and a pint of the very best brandy poured in. Two cups of firm red-ripe strawberries are sliced in half and added to the brandy, then two cups of sugar on top. This is stirred gently every day with a long-handled wooden spoon until the sugar is dissolved. Next fresh pineapple is peeled, sliced, and cut into small wedges. Cherries, black and sweet red, are pitted and stirred in. Added, in season, with equal amounts of sugar are two cups each of raspberries, left whole; then blackberries; apricots, quartered; peaches cut in generous cubes after skins have been removed. This is all stirred carefully after each addition until sugar has melted in. Several thicknesses of cheesecloth laid across the mouth of the jar, with the lid on top, keep out fruit flies. This is kept at least a month before tasting, to "marry" the fruit flavors. Grapes are too thick-skinned, pears and apples too bland to use. Blueberries, perhaps a handful, are sometimes added just for texture change, but they are apt to become tough-skinned and lose their individual flavor.

High on the top shelf of the butt'ry are the special-occasion dishes that are not used every day. The Canton-china punch bowl is carefully wrapped in tissue. The Turk's head mold for holiday cake-baking is there, and the turkey platter. Grandmother gave Grandfather that silver eggnog bowl on their silver wedding anniversary for serving his own special eggnog. This was the only thing he was ever known to step into the butt'ry to do, but this he did with a flourish and a disregard for the cost of rich ingredients that be-fitted the gracious Victorian gentleman. Hidden somewhere back of these things in those days were several bottles of what Grandmother called "special flavoring," which she used to put into special-occasion dishes of one kind or another, like plum pudding, fruit cake, and mincemeat; the bottles were not in plain sight in case a neighbor peeked into the butt'ry.

The spice chest doesn't begin to hold all the aromatic herbs and spices needed for good New England cooking, so they spill across the shelf in an array of highly decorative tins and jars and small wooden boxes labeled *Turmeric* and *Cardamom* and *Mace* and *Saffron* and *Marjoram* and many other romantic, pungent, spicy-sounding names.

A pepper grinder and a tin nutmeg grater sit beside the lovely smelling wooden lemon squeezer. The coffee mill is a two-wheeled generous one. In earlier days, green coffee beans were roasted in the oven just the proper amount, then fresh-ground for each pot. Now we buy already roasted beans mixed to order, and for special occasions there is a tin of S.S. Pierce's mocha-java always on hand.

Cooky molds of many shapes and sizes, mixing spoons and ladles with long handles, brass scoops, a rolling pin, and a copper cream skimmer hang here too. Worn and scratched from years of use are the butter paddles and chopping bowls of wood, a small cutting board with a sharp, sharp knife. The silvery sheen of pewter plates and measures contrasts with the warm yellow of the mixing crocks and cream pans.

There are eggs, carrots, and squashes brought up from the cellar. Rows of sparkling jellies and honey, a bag of nuts waiting to be cracked, a string of peppers and one of onions, bunches of herbs dried and ready to be hand-rubbed and stored in their proper painted tin canisters, and most are not kept more than a year. (The good New England housewife knows that the herbs and ground spices deteriorate.) There are always several bottles of vanilla in the making and one in use. A vanilla bean is sliced lengthwise, then cut in pieces with scissors and dropped into a six-ounce olive-green bottle full of rum, corked tightly and kept at least six months before using. Here is vanilla with taste and authority and none other is ever used. The vanilla sugar for flavoring whipped cream and frostings is made by cutting pieces of vanilla into a glass jar of sugar. The jar is then covered and the sugar is left to absorb the flavor for several weeks before it is used.

A necessity for lamb, the mint sauce is long-keeping and is true to its ancient symbolic herbal meaning of "eternal refreshment." We keep it in the butt'ry always in a green *crème de menthe* bottle, frequently made, frequently used. We boil together for twenty minutes 1½ cups sugar and 1½ cups good cider vinegar. A handful of spearmint is chopped very very fine

and added. It is then bottled and can be used within twenty-four hours or kept a long time.

Every inch of the butt'ry is crowded with goodness. Even the windowsill in winter is loaded in its sunshine with a pot of chives, a pot of parsley, and a rose geranium whose leaves are put into the bottom of the Lady Margaret Jane Cake tins to bake the delicate flavor into the best birthday cake of all. The Italian pottery jar that holds the rosemary plant was borne with care all the way from the marketplace in Orvieto in far-off Italy.

The most interesting place of all in the butt'ry is the shelf next to the kitchen door. It's easy to reach this shelf and even in the dark a searching hand can find and remove the proper reference when needed. For here is kept *The Buttery Book*, which is in fact a little collection of books containing traditional rules and receipts for cookery handed down and treasured and added to for many generations. The books vary in age and content and states of preservation, from an early-nineteenth-century *House-keeper's Book by a Lady* with its excellent instructions for building the kitchen-hearth fire and roasting meats on a spit to the old copybook with its handwritten and oft-changed family receipts to the latest edition of the *Calico Cook Book* compiled by our own church ladies' aid.

From all these books we find for ourselves, and now for you, the receipts for very special occasions. Many have been guarded, relished, and loved by family and good friends from Great-Grandmother's day. Some have never before been shared.

As the original *Buttery Book* receipts differed in their manner of being presented, so do the receipts which follow. Where the early rules often merely listed ingredients, we have tried to compose them so that they could be more easily followed by today's housewife and cook. Where the early rules called for general oven temperatures such as low, moderate, quick, or hot, we have tried to specify the Fahrenheit-degree temperatures we thought most nearly equal the desires of the originator of the receipt. This is also true of candy-making temperatures, which used to be soft-ball, hard-ball, and crack stages, but are much easier to achieve with correct temperature specifications.

Do share and enjoy with us in this *Butt'ry Shelf Cookbook* the fun and excitement of our family traditions for festive days.

New Year's Day Open House

RABBITS is the first word to be said on the first day every month. It's an old family custom, reputedly bringing money to anyone who doesn't forget to say it. The fact that it is sometimes hard to see that the promise comes true doesn't alter our fun in saying it. First to awaken, echoing through the house, begins the New Year with the magic word.

Nearly always a cold, cold day, sometimes quite a stormy one, this day in New England—and indeed the country over—is for family and friends of all sizes and ages. The old house is filled to bursting in spite of weather. Boots are stacked high in the front hall, the big four-poster bed in the company room is loaded with coats and caps and mittens. In the Old Kitchen, hot spiced cider is ready for passing in mugs as a good warm-up. This is a welcoming room with its huge fireplace, beehive oven, and blackened ceiling beams.

In the best parlor the candles have been lighted and the hearth-fire, too. Hot tea and coffee steam in gleaming silver pots reflecting the candlelight.

17

Beside the teapot are a pitcher of cream, a dish of lemon slices with clove, and one of candied mint leaves. On the coffee tray are a bowl of whipped cream and a silver nutmeg grater. Thin Staffordshire cups of green sprig pattern or pink luster, coin-silver teaspoons, and hand-hemstitched tea napkins are arranged on polished mahogany.

The Christmas Cooky Tree is loaded with the last and the best of the butt'ry holiday supply, now dwindled to these saved especially for this party. The traditional family Pound Cake is served on the best Sandwich-glass cake plate. A silver bread tray is brought to table, its neat rows of oh-so-thinly sliced Rich Plum Cake fragrant and glistening with "special flavoring." Grandfather's eggnog on the serving tables invites a toast to the New Year.

In the Old Kitchen, the children enjoy gingerbread animal cookies, and another mug of cider. Thin sandwiches disappear like magic. Have a look at the golden shining Christmas tree, and now "Happy New Year" is being called out everywhere until the last guest has gone. Candles have burned down and the last dish is washed. Back on the top shelf of the butt'ry go the Canton punch and silver eggnog bowls, and upstairs for us all, warmed by friendship and the fun of the New Year's first party.

NEW YEAR'S DAY OPEN HOUSE

Eggnog   Hot Spiced Cider

Christmas Cookies   Christmas Candies

Pound Cake   Rich Plum Cake

Date-Nut Bread Sandwiches

Gingerbread Animal Cookies

Tea   Candied Mint Leaves   Coffee

GRANDFATHER'S EGGNOG

Grandfather demanded full cooperation and attention from us all when he was ready to mix his eggnog. It was made in two important steps. The first step was the mixing of liquor, eggs, and milk. This was done the night before the party, then kept in a cold (not freezing) place until just before serving. The second step was beating the egg whites and cream and folding in the first mixture.

He presided at the serving bowl, and when all was ready, with a grand flourish he ladled the eggnog into cups, then grated nutmeg over each cupful, wishing each guest a Happy New Year. For the grating of the nutmeg, he used an eighteenth-century silver grater shaped like an acorn. His receipt was easy, rich, and delicious and served about twenty people.

1 dozen eggs	1 qt. heavy cream
1½ cups sugar	1 fifth good Bourbon whiskey
2 qts. rich milk	1 fifth good French cognac
1 tsp. salt	

Separate the eggs. Beat the yolks well until smooth. Beat in ½ cup of the sugar, add the milk, and beat well. Slowly pour in liquor and mix thoroughly. Pour into a gallon jug and keep in butt'ry or ice-box until just before serving time.

Then, in a bowl, beat room-temperature egg whites with a teaspoonful of salt until stiff enough to form peaks. Slowly add the remaining cup of sugar, still beating.

In the bottom of the chilled eggnog bowl, put the quart of heavy cream, which has been stiffly whipped. Combine the egg whites with the liquor mixture, then fold this into the whipped cream. Stir and dip and mix thoroughly with the silver ladle.

Serve in silver or glass punch cups. Grate nutmeg over each serving.

HOT SPICED CIDER

As long as there have been apples in New England there has been hot mulled cider, warming and hearty and healthful. Taverns in the old days served it with a good dollop of rum. Ours is a receipt for family and friends, warming enough without the tavern addition, especially on cold winter nights.

In a large kettle pour 1 gallon sweet cider; add and stir until dissolved 1 cup light brown sugar. In a small square of cheesecloth tie 2 sticks of cinnamon, 1 Tbs. whole cloves, 2 tsp. whole allspice. Drop this into cider and simmer for 20 minutes.

Warm a soup tureen and fill with the piping-hot brew (spices removed), then decorate with 2 or 3 floating lemon slices and whole cloves. Ladle into mugs. Or serve from a big pottery pitcher into mugs. Grate a touch of nutmeg over each serving if desired. Makes about 20 cups.

POUND CAKE

English Pound Cake was once called Twelfth Night Cake, but it is served now for any festive occasion. Old receipts called for a pound each of the ingredients, hence the name. Modern methods and materials have altered this somewhat. The mixing takes a lot of good beating, but with a light hand. It's helpful to have an assistant ready to take a spell at the mixing. Tradition bakes the cake in a Turk's head mold, but an angel-food tin is a suitable substitute. The cake is always sliced thin. Sometimes we serve Pound Cake for dessert with a ladleful of tutti-frutti sauce. Sometimes we serve ice cream on it. Mostly we relish it thin-sliced and eaten out of hand.

2 cups butter
2 generous cups sugar
10 eggs
2 Tbs. good cognac or brandy (or 2 tsp. vanilla or almond extract)

4 cups sifted flour
¼ tsp. salt
1 tsp. baking powder
1 tsp. mace

Beat softened butter with a wooden spoon until light. Add sugar and beat again until very light and fluffy. Beat eggs until light and add slowly to the butter, beating thoroughly and as lightly as you can after each addition. Add flavoring.

Mix salt, mace, baking powder with the flour. Fold, a cup at a time, into the butter mixture. Do this thoroughly so that flour is well incorporated, but lightly. Pour mixture into a well-buttered and lightly floured Turk's head mold.

Put in a cold oven, then bring to moderate (325°) heat. Bake for 1½ hours or longer until the cake is golden brown and has shrunk slightly from the side of the pan. It should test done when a knife-blade comes out clean. It will have a cracked top surface. Let cake stand to cool for ten minutes, then remove from pan to cake rack. When serving, dust lightly all over with powdered sugar. Cut into thin slices.

This cake may be wrapped in a cloth lightly moistened with brandy. It keeps for weeks on a shelf in the cool butt'ry or in the ice-box.

MISS IDA'S RICH PLUM CAKE

Miss Ida was our favorite aunt. A spinster lady with graceful hands that could paint or arrange a flower as successfully as tend them, she lived all her life in a little English town, but her interest in the world was very keen. Tea in her perfect garden or beside her sitting-room fire was a special occasion any day, but particularly so when an adoring visiting niece joined her. Her Rich Plum Cake has nary a plum in it, but plenty of other good things to make it the best of all our fruit cakes.

"Cream 8 ounces [1 cup] butter with a sturdy wooden spoon," she advised, then continued:

Add and cream well until light 8 oz. (1 cup) sugar. Add 5 eggs, which you have beaten till light, and mix well. Stir in: ¾ lb. (2½ cups) flour, a generous pinch (1 tsp.) cinnamon, a pinch of allspice (½ tsp.), a pinch of mace (½ tsp.).

Add: 6 oz. mixed chopped candied peel, 6 oz. glacé cherries cut in halves, ½ lb. Sultanas (seeded white raisins will do), 3 oz. (⅓ to ½ cup) chopped almonds. Add a wineglass (½ cup) of good brandy and mix all well together.

Put the mixture into a very well-greased and floured baking pan (Turk's head mold) and bake in a slow oven (325°) for 1½ hours. Then bake for another ½ hour at an even lower temperature (300°).

Remove from oven, cool for ten or fifteen minutes, and remove from pan.

ICINGS FOR RICH PLUM CAKE

There are two icings for the cake. The first to go on is the *Almond Icing.*

Use ½ lb. ground almonds (or almond paste). Add the beaten yolk of 1 egg, then the beaten white. Add ½ lb. (1¾ cup) of powdered sugar and a few drops of lemon juice.

With a knife dipped in cold water, spread the almond icing on the cake, adding a drop or two of water if necessary to make of spreading consistency. Keep dipping knife to make frosting go on easily. Dry overnight before applying the second frosting.

The *White Icing* is made by combining 1 lb. powdered sugar with the beaten whites of 2 eggs and the juice of 1 lemon. Beat with a wooden spoon until smooth. Dip knife in cold water and spread over the almond icing, working carefully. Cover completely with the white icing. Decorate with cherries, pistachio nuts, sugared flowers and leaves, angelica, "or anything you fancy."

DATE-NUT BREAD SANDWICHES

First, of course, make the date-nut bread:

3 cups sifted flour	1 beaten large egg
3 tsp. baking powder	¾ cup heavy sour cream
¼ tsp. soda	¾ cup milk
1 tsp. mace	¼ cup melted butter
1 tsp. salt	2 tsp. grated orange rind
½ cup white sugar	½ cup chopped butternuts, walnuts, or
½ cup brown sugar	pecans
	1 cup chopped dates

Sift flour again with baking powder, soda, mace, salt, and sugars. Combine egg, milk, and cream and stir into flour, then add butter, grated rind and mix together. Fold in nuts and dates. Turn into well-greased 9-inch loaf pan and let stand for a few minutes while oven is heated (to 350°). Bake about an hour, or until the bread tests done with straw or thin knife-blade. Cool. Remove from pan and wrap in foil and store at least overnight before slicing.

To make sandwiches, spread one-half of the thin sliced pieces with butter, the other half with softened cream cheese. Put together in pairs, cut some in half diagonally; cut some in long narrow "fingers," and arrange on a doily on a plate.

GINGERBREAD ANIMAL COOKIES

1 cup butter	6 cups flour
1 cup light brown sugar	1½ Tbs. ginger
3 eggs, well beaten	2 tsp. salt
1½ cups molasses	1½ tsp. soda
	1 tsp. cinnamon

Cream butter; add sugar, egg, molasses, and flour mixed with dry ingredients. Chill and roll out and cut with cooky cutter or cut around cardboard animal shapes with a knife. If they are to be hung on the Cooky Tree, thread clean string with a darning needle through the top of the cooky before baking. Bake in a moderate oven (350°) about 10 minutes. Do not overbake. This makes many cookies; the actual number depends on their size. When cookies are cool outline with frosting in a cornucopia (or decorating tube).

To make frosting, beat 1 egg white very stiff. Over this pour boiling syrup made from ¾ cup sugar and ¼ cup water boiled until it spins a thread. Mix well and pipe onto cookies.

CANDIED MINT LEAVES

Violets, Johnny-jump-ups, rose petals (or whole single Scotch roses), mint leaves, or herb leaves of any dainty fragrance may be crystallized on a dry cool day and stored in separate tight jars for use in ornamenting cakes, cookies, ice cream, or the tea table.

Gather the flowers and leaves, preferably when they have dried just after a rain for freshness and best flavor. Choose them carefully and make sure there are no specks of dirt or insects, washing if necessary. Dry, separated, on paper towels.

For a generous handful of leaves, beat one or two egg whites with one tablespoon of water until blended. Stir in flavoring: 2 or 3 drops of almond for violets; peppermint oil for mint leaves; lemon extract for rose or lemon verbena or scented geranium leaves.

With a clean half-inch-wide camel's-hair paint brush, apply the egg white to leaves or flowers, covering thoroughly. Or dip carefully with tweezers. Spread ½ cup white sugar in a flat dish (more as needed), and as leaves are dipped in egg white, dip them quickly into sugar, again covering well. Place separately on wax paper on a cooky sheet and dry in the sun or a slow oven (200°) for about 30 minutes. Store in layers (with wax paper between layers) in covered glass jars.

Valentine's Day

FOR at least a week before February 14 the house is cluttered with a delightful muss of paper doilies, red-paper hearts, bits of gilt paper and colored ribbons, pictures of cupids and arrows, and forget-me-nots and roses and violets. A glass jar filled with sugar candy hearts spills "I Love You" and "Be Mine" over the kitchen table. Everybody is asking for scissors and paste.

We make a "post-office box" to take to school and cover it with shiny red paper, decorate it with some of the lace and ribbon and crêpe-paper ruffles, then cut a slit in the top so that the children in the schoolroom can "mail" their envelopes filled with sentiment for the teacher and others.

There is a post-office box for home, too, one of Mother's hat boxes covered with wallpaper with big red roses on it. This is for our own Valentine's Day party, after school, when the neighborhood children come with their masterpieces. Some giggling, some blushing, some solemn posting of letters; then the games begin, the party lunch is served, and—most exciting of all—the mail is distributed. More giggles, of course some tears. But Mother is the postman and she has made sure that everyone has a beautiful Valentine before going home.

The day is not over, for on the dinner table are red roses in a silver bowl, red candles alight, and a place card, which is Mother's special Valentine to each of us. There is a big pink Valentine cake for family dessert, and then Father springs a "surprise"—each year the same but each year still a surprise—when he brings out a tremendous red-satin heart box for Mother, filled with the best boughten candy to be found at the Corner Drug Store in town.

VALENTINE'S DAY PARTY

Open-faced Heart-shaped Sandwiches
spread with
Raspberry Jam and Cream Cheese, Peanut Butter and Currant Jelly
Banana Bread Sandwiches
Sugar Cooky Hearts
Eben's Pink Peppermint Stick Ice Cream
Cold Milk in sparkling glass punch cups served from
the punch bowl

AT DINNER

Pink Valentine's Day Cake with shredded coconut

BANANA BREAD

½ cup butter
½ cup light brown sugar
½ cup white sugar
3 Tbs. sour cream
2 eggs, well beaten
1 cup mashed ripe bananas
Grated rind of 1 orange

2 cups flour
1 tsp. baking powder
½ tsp. soda
¼ tsp. salt
½ tsp. mace
½ cup chopped walnuts or
    pecans

Cream softened (but not melted) butter. Add sugar, creaming until well blended. Add sour cream. Stir eggs into creamed mixture; add orange rind. Sift together the dry ingredients and add to the creamed mixture alternately with the mashed bananas. Fold in nuts.

Pour into a well-greased loaf pan and bake in a medium oven (350°) about 50 to 60 minutes, or until knife stuck in center comes out clean.

When cool, wrap loaf in foil and let stand overnight. Slice thinly, spread with soft butter and make sandwiches, cutting in halves or quarters crosswise.

MOTHER'S SUGAR COOKIES

1 cup sugar
½ cup butter
2 eggs, well beaten
1 cup heavy sour cream
1 Tbs. vanilla
1 tsp. almond flavoring

2¾ cups flour
1 tsp. salt
½ of a nutmeg, grated
1 tsp. baking powder
½ tsp. soda

Cream butter and sugar together. Add eggs and cream. Add flavorings. Sift dry ingredients and add to other mixture. Chill. Divide into several pieces and roll out one at a time. Roll thin on floured board; cut with heart-shaped cooky cutter. Sprinkle generously with pink or red sugar after placing on cooky sheet. Bake in medium oven (350°) until delicately brown. Watch carefully so as not to brown too much. Makes about 75 cookies.

EBEN'S PINK PEPPERMINT STICK ICE CREAM

1½ cups sugar	3 cups heavy cream
1¾ qt. milk	5 eggs, well beaten

Combine the ingredients and scald just until the mixture coats the spoon. Remove from fire, add 1 tsp. peppermint extract and several drops of red food coloring. Chill. Pour into freezer can. When the cream is about half frozen (when you begin to feel a slight pull in the cranking), add 1½ cups crushed peppermint stick candy. This will leave bits of candy for texture in the ice cream. Makes 3 quarts.

VALENTINE'S DAY CAKE

½ cup butter	1 cup milk
1½ cups sugar	1 tsp. vanilla
2½ cups cake flour	½ tsp. almond extract
2½ tsp. baking powder	4 egg whites

With a wooden spoon, cream together the butter and sugar and beat until light and fluffy. Sift dry ingredients together and add to the creamed mixture alternately with the milk. Add vanilla and almond. Beat the egg whites until stiff and fold in lightly.

Butter and lightly flour an 8-inch angel-food pan or two 8-inch layer pans. Pour in the batter and bake in moderate (350°) oven for 30 to 35 minutes or until cake springs back when touched lightly with the finger. Let rest a few minutes, then turn onto wire rack to cool.

For a larger cake, double the receipt and make in four 8-inch layer pans.

PINK FROSTING FOR VALENTINE'S DAY CAKE

In a saucepan mix ½ cup sugar, 2 Tbs. water, and ½ cup light corn syrup. Cover saucepan and bring to a rolling boil. Remove cover and cook until syrup spins a thread at least 6 inches long (242° on candy thermometer). Turn off heat.

Beat 2 egg whites (¼ cup) until stiff enough to hold peaks. Pour the hot syrup very slowly into the beaten egg whites. Continue to beat until frosting holds peaks; blend in 1 tsp. vanilla and some red food coloring to make a pretty pink color. Spread on cooled cake in soft swirls.

To make pink coconut for dusting the frosting, add red food coloring to 1 Tbs. water in a quart jar. Add a cupful of shredded coconut, cover the jar and shake vigorously until all coconut is colored. Spread on paper toweling to dry. Pat carefully onto sides of Valentine Cake. It is best to color the coconut before starting to make the frosting, so it can be put on before frosting sets.

Easter Sunday

GETTING-UP time is early on Easter morning; everyone is up to have first choice of beribboned egg baskets and to hunt colored eggs, for the one who finds the most has first slice of the Easter cake on the sideboard awaiting dinner. Presents are hidden, too, and when the last one is found, breakfast is served. In the center of the big table is the Easter-egg tree, banked with geraniums and hyacinths in pots. Eggshells for the tree are lavishly decorated with gold and pearls and lace ribbons; some have windows looking into miniature scenes of great ingenuity and beauty. (Can we have seen these hanging on the Christmas tree, too?) Each year a few new ones appear on Easter morning. The trimmings have been saved in a special box as they are collected the whole year through—bits of braid, some tiny buttons, diminutive cutout figures of children, trees, houses, animals, birds and butterflies small enough to fit inside the egg-shell.

We take plenty of time to enjoy Easter breakfast, then off to Sunday school and church, with a new bonnet or necktie or white kid gloves, everyone with a boutonnière from Father of a single fresh flower to signify our joy in this Easter Day.

Home from church, the ice-cream freezer is scalded and filled, ice is pounded in a burlap bag, salt is poured on, and anyone who doesn't take a turn with the freezing doesn't get to scrape the dasher. Then we pack the freezer carefully with more ice and salt, cover with plenty of newspapers and a clean piece of blanket or towels to await dinner. Old-fashioned long-cured ham has been boiled and now is put into the oven to bake, then scored, studded with cloves, and glazed with maple syrup and apple cider.

Many years ago, the Easter cake was a graduated four-layer one made just for us by the German baker in town. He had no family of his own and it became his labor of love at Eastertime to outdo all other Easter cakes. There were tiny frosting chickens and ducks and lambs, birds and butterflies, an angel or two, and many delicately wrought frosting flowers and vines. On the very top was a little cottage of cake and frosting with a fence and roses climbing over the door. The top three layers were carefully removed at the dinner table (Do be careful, don't break it!) and put back into the paper cake box. On the morrow, in turns each year, the children took it to school to share with their classmates. The family ate the festooned bottom layer. The baker has long gone and our cake today is not the glorious creation he would have made of it, but we still yellow-frost our lemon sponge Easter cake and do our best with the decorations.

The table is set with Great-Grandma's lily-of-the-valley damask linen with matching yard-square napkins. Dishes are Haviland of the pink rosebud pattern, goblets of the New England pineapple pattern, symbol of hospitality—and relatives and friends often share this day and this meal with us.

EASTER BREAKFAST

Fresh Fruit in Grapefruit Baskets
A Mountain of Curried Scrambled Eggs
Home-made Sausage   Hot Cross Buns
Pot of Coffee   Hot Chocolate

EASTER DINNER

Jellied Chicken Consommé with Mint Sprig
Baked Ham with Maple Syrup and Cider Glaze
garnished with
Easter Eggs in Parsley Nests
Corn Pudding   Au Gratin Potatoes   Perfection Salad
Orange Twists
Vanilla Ice Cream with Tutti-Frutti
Lemon Sponge Easter Cake

Easter Breakfast

FRESH FRUIT IN GRAPEFRUIT BASKETS

For each two persons cut one grapefruit in half. Cut out sections and put in a large bowl. With sharp knife and fingers, pull out the membranes, leaving a smooth interior. Notch edges of each half with sharp scissors or knife.

To the grapefruit sections in the large bowl add sections of oranges (allowing about half an orange to a person), cubes of fresh pineapple, one can of drained apricot halves, some strawberries, some seeded fresh grapes or whatever good fresh fruit is obtainable. Add enough juice from the apricots to provide some syrup, and chill overnight.

In the morning, spoon into grapefruit baskets, garnish with fresh grated coconut and with fresh or candied mint leaves; add a teaspoon of kirsch to the grown-ups' baskets.

A MOUNTAIN OF CURRIED SCRAMBLED EGGS

For eight people: into a large mixing bowl break a dozen eggs. Add 1½ tsp. salt and a good grinding of black pepper. Add 2 tsp. curry powder. Beat lightly, then add ⅓ cup rich milk and blend.

Put a lump of butter the size of a jumbo egg into a large frying pan and melt, turning the pan to coat it well with the butter. Pour in the eggs, cooking slowly. Stir only occasionally as the eggs set. When set and still shiny, not dry, pile up in the center of a hot platter, surround with home-made sausage patties or links, garnish with watercress or parsley, and serve.

HOMEMADE SAUSAGE

Sausage can be made at any time of the year by buying the pork at the butcher's and having him grind it. We do it at butchering time and make a party of it. Rosie and Lulu are invariably the names of the pigs, raised on grain, skim milk, apples.

For fifteen pounds of sausage, we allow ¼ to ⅓ fat; the rest is good lean meat and scraps of meat. Grind about 15 pounds of meat and fat together into a large dishpan (or two dishpans). Have the seasonings prepared and scatter over the sausage as it comes from the grinder. Then stir lightly and work with the hands until seasonings are well mixed in. Fry a panful of patties; everyone tastes the seasoning.

With a sausage stuffer (well scalded beforehand), feed sausage through into casings (which can be bought from a wholesale meat market and often from a butcher), twisting into links of whatever length you prefer. Or shape into rolls of about a pound each and wrap in foil. Freeze the sausage. To serve, thaw first, then slice and fry.

SEASONING FOR 15 LBS. SAUSAGE

¼ cup salt
3 Tbs. fresh ground
    black pepper
4 Tbs. dried sage

2 Tbs. combined thyme and summer
    savory
2 Tbs. marjoram

The herbs may be dried or fresh. If fresh, allow about one-half more, since dried herbs are stronger than fresh.

HOT CROSS BUNS

2 pkgs. powdered yeast
⅓ cup warm water
⅓ cup scalded milk
½ cup butter
⅓ cup sugar

¾ tsp. salt
3½ to 4 cups flour
1 tsp. cinnamon
3 well-beaten eggs
⅔ cup dried currants

Soften yeast in water. Into the scalded milk, stir the butter, sugar, and salt; let cool to lukewarm in a large bowl.

Sift flour and cinnamon together. Into the milk mixture, stir a cup of flour and mix well. Add eggs and beat well, then add the softened yeast and the currants. Add the remaining flour, a cup or so at a time, and mix thoroughly to make a soft dough. Cover with a clean dampened towel and let rise in a warm place until double, 1½ to 2 hours. Punch down.

Roll dough ½ inch thick on a lightly floured board. Cut into rounds with a biscuit or cooky cutter and shape into 24 rounded buns. Place well apart on a greased baking sheet. Cover and let rise in a warm place for an hour. With a sharp knife or scissors, cut a cross in the center of each bun. Brush tops with egg white or milk. Bake in moderately hot oven (375°) about 12 minutes or until nicely browned.

Remove from oven and pipe or dribble white frosting on buns to make a cross. Frosting is made by stirring together until smooth 1 lightly beaten egg white and enough powdered sugar to make a paste (¾ to 1 cup); add ½ tsp. vanilla.

POT OF COFFEE

The family's favorite breakfast coffee is made in a granite (enamelware) coffee pot. In the bottom of the pot put a heaping tablespoon of freshly ground coffee per cup of water, plus one tablespoon for the pot if you like hearty coffee. Onto this, pour the yolk and white of an egg and shake the pot vigorously for a minute to combine. Pour measured boiling water over this, then let it boil on the stove for about a minute. Pour in a cup of cold water and let stand on the back of the stove (or turn down the heat) to allow the grounds to settle for a few minutes. Allow a half cup of water per serving.

OLD-FASHIONED HOT CHOCOLATE

3 squares unsweetened chocolate	½ tsp. salt
⅔ cup water	½ cup heavy cream, whipped
1 cup sugar	5 cups scalded milk

Melt chocolate and water over low heat in a large saucepan, stirring to mix. Add sugar and salt and stir well. Bring to a simmer and cook 4 or

5 minutes. Cool slightly, then fold in whipped cream. When ready to serve, pour into a heated pitcher or chocolate pot. Add the hot milk slowly, stirring well, and pour into cups. Top with a marshmallow if desired.

Easter Dinner

JELLIED CHICKEN CONSOMMÉ WITH MINT SPRIG

Into a large kettle, put a 4- or 5-pound fowl and cover with about 3 quarts of cold water. Bring to a boil and simmer gently for two hours or until tender, adding to the water:

1 tsp. salt
Handful of finely chopped
    parsley sprigs

1 cup chopped celery and celery
    leaves
½ cup chopped onion
1 bay leaf

When meat is tender, take from stove and allow the chicken to cool in the broth. Remove chicken and separate the meat from bones and skin. Use the meat for salad or pie. Put bones and skin back into the kettle and simmer for another half hour or longer. Strain the broth into a bowl, taste for seasoning, cool and remove the fat from the top. Chill thoroughly.

When ready to serve, place a half thin-cut lemon slice in the bottom of a consommé cup, spoon chilled broth on top, and decorate with a small mint sprig.

BAKED HAM WITH MAPLE SYRUP AND CIDER GLAZE

Soak a country cured and smoked ham overnight in cold water. When ready to boil, scrub in cold water with a vegetable brush. Put into a large pot. Cover the ham with water to which 2 cups good cider have been added. Bring to a boil and simmer gently 15 minutes per pound. Allow it to cool in the cooking water. Remove from kettle and cut off heavy skin, allowing a strip to remain on the shank end, cutting into points if desired for appearance.

Put the ham into an open roasting pan and brush with a mixture made of ½ cup maple syrup and ¼ cup sweet cider. Bake in a slow oven (325°) for an hour, basting frequently with the syrup mixture. Remove from oven, score with a knife diagonally in two directions, stud with cloves, brush again with syrup, and return to the oven for an additional 20 minutes.

Place on hot platter and garnish with bunches of parsley onto which colored or decorated Easter eggs have been placed.

CORN PUDDING

2 cups drained whole kernel yellow corn
1 tsp. salt
2 tsp. sugar
¼ tsp. freshly ground pepper
2 well-beaten eggs
1 cup rich milk
1 tsp. Worcestershire sauce
2 Tbs. melted butter
2 or 3 Tbs. finely crumbled cracker crumbs

Combine all ingredients except crumbs and mix well. Pour into a one-quart attractive baking dish. Scatter crumbs over the top. Set in a pan in water an inch deep and bake in a moderate oven (350°) for 60 minutes or until a knife inserted into the center comes out clean. Serve from dish in which pudding is baked.

AU GRATIN POTATOES

Boil, in salted water to cover, one medium-sized potato per person. When cool enough to handle, peel and slice thinly into a buttered casserole.

Make a medium cream sauce: Melt 1 Tbs. butter, add 1 Tbs. flour, cook and stir until bubbly. Stir in slowly 1 cup rich milk; continue to cook and stir until thickened. Remove from heat and add ½ tsp. salt and a pinch of cayenne pepper. Add ½ tsp. dry mustard that has been mixed with a little milk. Slowly add 1 cup grated sharp cheese and stir until melted.

Pour the cheese sauce over the potatoes. Sprinkle some grated cheese over the top. Bake in a medium oven (350°) until well browned, 20 to 30 minutes.

PERFECTION SALAD

Make a gelatin using one package of either lemon or lime gelatin and set aside to cool but not set hard.

Add 2 Tbs. lemon juice or good cider vinegar to the following:

1 cup finely shredded crisp cabbage
½ cup shredded carrot
½ cup finely chopped celery
¼ cup chopped green pepper
5 or 6 finely chopped sweet pickles
1 tsp. salt

When gelatin is cool and just beginning to set, add vegetables and stir in well. Pour into a ring mold or into eight individual molds. Chill until firm. When ready to serve, unmold onto salad plates and garnish with lettuce. Serve with mayonnaise.

ORANGE TWISTS

Orange twists disappear so fast that we have sometimes doubled the receipt. The following rule makes 1½ dozen twists.

Sift together 2 cups flour, 3 tsp. baking powder, and 1 tsp. salt. With knives or pastry blender, cut in 4 Tbs. firm butter. Add ⅔ cup milk or slightly more, and stir to make a soft dough.

Turn onto a lightly floured board and knead for half a minute. Pat or roll into a rectangle about 8x12 inches wide and ½ inch thick. Spread over the dough and roll in well a mixture of 2 Tbs. sugar and the grated rind of one good-sized orange. Cut the dough into strips 8 inches long by about ⅜ inches wide; fold over to double, then twist. Place on a greased baking sheet, firming the ends so the dough will not untwist. Bake in a hot oven (450°) for 10 or 12 minutes, until nicely browned. The twists may be brushed with milk and sugared before baking. Serve hot in a basket lined with a linen napkin.

LEMON SPONGE CAKE

This is a festive cake at any time, baked in an angel-food pan. For Easter, we bake it in two 9-inch layer-cake pans and decorate it with Lemon Butter Frosting topped with sugared flowers and leaves.

Grease the bottoms of two 9-inch layer-cake pans and dust lightly with flour.

6 eggs, separated	1 tsp. vanilla
⅛ tsp. salt	Grated rind of 1 lemon
1⅛ cups superfine sugar	1 Tbs. lemon juice
1 cup sifted cake flour	

Beat the egg whites and salt together until soft peaks form. Beat in the sugar, a little at a time, until whites are very stiff. Beat the egg yolks thoroughly. Add lemon juice, lemon rind, and vanilla.

Into the yolks, fold about a cupful of the beaten whites. Continue folding until well mixed. Sift in the flour and fold all lightly together, using a wooden spoon.

Turn mixture into the pans and level the tops. Hit pans sharply on table to settle. Bake in a moderate oven (350°) until top springs back when pressed lightly with finger. Cool on cake racks.

LEMON BUTTER FROSTING

¼ lb. soft butter	1 egg
About 4 cups sifted powdered sugar	Grated rind of 1 lemon
⅛ tsp. salt	2 Tbs. lemon juice
	Few drops yellow food coloring

Cream the butter until light. Add about a cup of the powdered sugar gradually, beating until smooth. Add egg and lemon rind and beat well, then add more sugar alternately with lemon juice and beat well each time, until the right consistency for spreading. Add yellow food coloring and mix in thoroughly.

COUNTRY VANILLA ICE CREAM

4 eggs, beaten in a large bowl	5 cups cold milk
2¼ cups sugar	4 cups cold heavy cream
½ tsp. salt	5 tsp. vanilla

Add sugar to the beaten eggs gradually. Beat until the mixture is stiff and thoroughly mixed. Add milk, cream, and vanilla. Mix thoroughly and pour into a gallon freezer. After freezing, pack in ice and salt and let stand for several hours. Serve with tutti-frutti or other sauce.

May Basket Day

MAY Basket Day is as pretty a custom as children have ever known but one to which modern children pay little attention. What excitement they miss! There is the gathering of all the materials to make the baskets, and again the house is cluttered with colored paper, ribbons and such. Ingenuity (with some help from big sisters) makes a gay assortment of baskets. Cornucopias of wallpaper are favorites. Some baskets are woven of sturdy paper and decorated with ribbon. Berry baskets and ice-cream cartons make good foundations for May baskets, filled with candy and cookies and a nosegay peeking out at the top, each with a strong handle of ribbon, the better to hang on doorknobs.

The butt'ry is crowded, for everyone helps as Mother makes the cookies. There are several kinds of favorites by special request, including her special Sugar Cookies. As she mixes the dough and rolls it out on the board, then flips cutouts onto a cooky sheet to be carried by small willing hands into the kitchen for popping into a ready oven, she sings an unforgettable verse from an old song book.

MOTHER MAKING COOKIES

1. O, what fun it is to be   In the Butt'ry just to see
2. How they smell and how they look When she puts them in to cook.
3. Round and shin-ing on the top,   I   can hard-ly e-ver stop

1. Mo - ther mak-ing coo-kies, Mo - ther mak-ing   cook - ies!
2. O,   how   I love coo-kies! O,   how   I   love   cook- ies!
3. Eat - ing such good coo -kies, Eat - ing Mo-ther's   cook -ies!

Summer is almost here; celebrate it with May Basket Day. Make plenty of cookies and candy and gather the prettiest flowers—pansies from the garden, violets from the fields and woods. Find the fragrant pink Mayflower for the best basket, and fill it to overflowing. Ring a doorbell, then run and hide, leaving someone who comes to the door to wonder and guess who could have made such a pretty basket full of goodies.

After school we gather young friends for the Maypole Party. Into the attic in an excited rush to pull from the cedar chest pretty dresses, hats, and slippers of another era for little girls to dress up in. From an old sea chest come fancy waistcoats and knee pants and soldiers' uniforms for little boys to wear. One could never suspect that the Maypole was yesterday a clothes pole, for now it is wound with gay crêpe-paper ribbons. The melodeon has been moved to the front hall, the door is open wide, and sister Margaret plays as we sing and dance and wind the ribbons, stumbling sometimes in too-long dress-up skirts and too-big boots.

Then dash for the punch table. There is a-plenty of cookies and punch.

Mother's Sugar Cookies (p. 29)

Frosty Ginger Creams   Dipsy Do's

Coconut Kisses   Pecan Dreamies

Peanut Butter Cookies

Punch

FROSTY GINGER CREAMS

½ cup sugar	1 tsp. ginger
⅓ cup butter	½ tsp. nutmeg
1 egg	½ tsp. powdered cloves
½ cup molasses	½ tsp. cinnamon
½ cup water	½ tsp. salt
2 cups sifted flour	½ tsp. soda

Cream butter and sugar together; add egg, molasses, and water and mix together thoroughly until smooth. Sift all dry ingredients together and add to the creamed mixture. Put in ice-box to chill for at least an hour.

Drop dough well apart by teaspoonful on greased cooky sheet. Bake in a hot oven (400°) for 8 to 10 minutes. Allow to cool on cooky sheet for a minute, then remove to cake rack with spatula. Frost with lemon icing.

LEMON ICING

Beat 1 egg white until stiff. Gradually beat in about ½ cup powdered sugar, a pinch of salt, and the grated rind of a lemon. Stir until smooth; spread over ginger cookies.

DIPSY DO'S

Crack pecans, walnuts, butternuts, hazelnuts, or almonds, keeping them in whole or half form as much as possible. Have ready small pieces of candied ginger, candied fruit peel, candied cherries, caramels, peppermints, or little balls of fondant (p. 173).

Melt slowly over warm, not hot, water, 8 ounces of sweet, semisweet, or bitter chocolate, as you prefer. Add 4 Tbs. butter and a 1-by-2-inch piece of the paraffin you keep on hand for sealing jelly jars. Melt slowly, stir, and add about ½ tsp. vanilla. Remove from heat and cool a little but do not let it get cold or congeal. To keep it soft, the mixture may be put over a pan of warm water. Using tweezers or tongs, dip the nuts or other pieces that you have ready. Put on marble slab or cold platter to harden and cool.

PECAN DREAMIES

There are never enough of these cookies. They are made for almost every special occasion, tea parties especially. The trouble is they are eaten by the handful, not by the cooky.

1 cup butter	½ tsp. almond or maple flavoring
¼ cup sugar	2 cups flour
2 tsp. vanilla	2 cups ground pecans

With wooden spoon, cream butter and sugar together, and add flavorings. Add flour, then nuts. Mold by teaspoonsful into small balls or crescents and arrange on cooky sheet. Flatten slightly with a fork. Bake in moderately hot oven (375°) until delicately brown; do not overbake. Remove from oven and while still warm roll in a dish of powdered sugar; shake off excess and cool.

PEANUT BUTTER COOKIES

½ cup soft butter	2 eggs, beaten
½ cup margarine	2½ cups flour
1 cup peanut butter	½ tsp. salt
1 cup brown sugar	2 tsp. soda
1 cup white sugar	1 tsp. baking powder

Cream shortenings and peanut butter together, beat in brown and white sugar, then mix in beaten eggs. Sift dry ingredients together and add to the creamed mixture. Roll dough into small balls about an inch in diameter, place well apart on a lightly greased cooky sheet, and flatten with a fork. Place a half peanut in the center of each. Bake in moderately hot oven (375°) for 10 or 12 minutes, until lightly browned. Do not overbake.

COCONUT KISSES

Cut 2 pieces of brown wrapping paper and fit over two cooky sheets.

Beat a half-cup (about four) egg whites until frothy. Gradually beat in 1¼ cups sugar, then continue beating until mixture is very stiff. Stir in a pinch of salt and ½ tsp. almond flavoring. Fold in about 2½ cups of shredded coconut.

Divide mixture into four bowls and tint three different colors, leaving one white. Then drop half-teaspoonfuls of mixture an inch apart on the cooky sheets. Bake in slow oven (300°) about 30 minutes or until set and very delicately browned.

Remove from oven and (working quickly) slide brown paper off cooky sheet, lay a wet dishtowel on hot cooky sheet, and slide the brown paper back over it. The moisture in the towel penetrates the paper and the meringues may easily be removed with a spatula. Cool thoroughly on cake racks. Makes 60 or 70 bite-size kisses.

MAYPOLE PUNCH

4 qts. pineapple juice	Juice of 6 oranges
1 qt. cranberry juice cocktail	Juice of 3 lemons
	2 cups sugar, or to taste
1 bottle Rose's lime juice (sweetened)	2 qts. ginger ale
	2 qts. soda water

Mix fruit juices together and add sugar, stirring well to dissolve sugar. Chill thoroughly. When ready to serve, place a piece of ice in the punch bowl, pour the fruit juices over it. Add the ginger ale and soda water. Garnish with slices of orange stuck with a clove. Serve in punch cups with a stick of striped peppermint candy for stirring. This receipt will provide about three gallons of punch.

Afternoon Tea Parties

THE garden is at its welcoming best in spring, with "a host of golden daffodils" in the border and rock gardens and growing naturally in the fields. Grape hyacinths edge the door-rock, and one can see squill and early tulips and violets (who can bear to pull up a violet which makes the spring borders so gay, and acts as lush green ground-cover all summer long?). Kitten-faces on violas and pansies nod under the blossoming cherry and crab-apple trees. Lilacs have budded and perennial beds are blanketed with swift-growing plants.

The bronze fountain figure in a corner of the spring bulb garden splashes happily in the old soapstone sink sunk into the ground and edged with lilies-of-the-valley. (We rescued this figure from a trash heap.) Nearby the tiny hand-carved St. Francis bought in a courtyard shop in Innsbruck bows his head in a blessing of the many nesting birds.

We get out the garden benches from winter storage, paint them, and don't forget to put one down at the end of the lane for birdwatching. We turn the compost, uncover the roses, mow the lawn.

There is no resisting a garden party to share this springtime loveliness, and so invite friends and neighbors and garden-club ladies to walk at leisure around the garden. They take copious notes; they lift eyebrows at hurry-up garden tidying and they compare varieties. We're sorry if some of the labels are mixed up—our small corgi Stedly Alexander prefers chewing garden labels to almost anything else and has his own way of distributing them along the borders.

We have put away the winter doors to the summer kitchen and now fill the plant stands there with geraniums pink and red and salmon and white, and with house plants to face the warming sun. We set the long pine harvest table in this spacious open room with a brown bowl of spring flowers; with brown-and-white china with which Mother started house-keeping; with napkins woven on the eighteenth-century loom in our own weaving room. Fill the copper teakettle on the summer-kitchen stove and bring it just to the boil; take from the oven the pans of gingerbread. Serve the hot and fragrant spicy tea from an old Bennington teapot, and enjoy a country tea party in the spring.

SPRING TEA PARTY

Hot Gingerbread
with Plenty of Home-made Butter
or Whipped Cream or Maple Cream
Spiced Tea

Gingerbread was our annual entry to the County Fair and we always won a seventy-five-cent first prize, a lot of money to a little girl years ago. (It was the only gingerbread there!) The best gingerbread for tea parties is baked in old-fashioned iron gem pans.

GINGERBREAD

½ cup sugar	2½ cups sifted flour
½ cup butter	1½ tsp. soda
1 egg, beaten	1 tsp. cinnamon
1 cup molasses	1 tsp. ginger
1 cup hot water	½ tsp. powdered cloves
1½ cups raisins	½ tsp. salt

Cream butter and sugar together, add beaten egg and the molasses. Then add dry ingredients sifted together. Add hot water and beat until smooth. Fold in the raisins. Bake in well-buttered gem pans (or in a loaf or cake pan) in a medium oven (350°) until it tests done with a broom-straw. This makes 24 gems.

MAPLE CREAM

A wonderful addition to hot gingerbread, hot biscuits or spice cake, or on a slice of bread for after-school lunches, Maple Cream can be kept for days in the ice-box.

For the family, to serve four or five, stir together (in a Bennington bowl, of course) 1 cup heavy sour cream and ¼ cup maple syrup with a pinch of salt. Put in a sauceboat and grate nutmeg over the top. Chill thoroughly.

For a tea party with perhaps twenty ladies, use 4 cups of sour cream, a cup of maple syrup, and ½ tsp. salt. Grate nutmeg over the top and chill before serving.

SPICED TEA

Before the guests are due to arrive, put in a saucepan 1 cup white sugar, 1 cup water, 4 whole cinnamon sticks, 1 Tbs. whole cloves, and the grated rind of 1 lemon and 1 orange. Boil for five minutes, stirring to dissolve sugar, then remove cinnamon sticks and cloves. Add 1 cup orange juice, 6 Tbs. lemon juice, and 1 cup pineapple juice. Stir well.

At serving time, pour 3 qts. boiling water over 12 tsp. tea (or teabags if you must) and steep about 5 minutes. Stir, strain, and combine with the heated juice mixture. Serve from a brown teapot or a large Bennington bowl into cups or little brown mugs. The cupfuls may be garnished with ¼ slice lemon and 1 clove for a special touch, or drop a single mint leaf into each cup. This will serve twenty.

On a sunny summer's day, the place for an afternoon tea party with friends who will enjoy the color in the borders is in the arbor. It is shaded by an ancient grapevine, dripping with fuchsias in hanging baskets, and lined with potted geraniums. The ice-cream table is covered with a gay checked cloth; spoons and tea knives are in a basket. We fill a cut-glass pitcher with minted iced tea. A bowl of raspberries or strawberries or blackberries, picked with the hulls left on, is ready for dipping one by one into superfine sugar. Thin crisp brownies are fresh from the oven. Sandwiches are paper-thin, too, delicate to taste and dainty to see. "Plain Cake," round and plump, is frosty with powdered sugar and ringed with field daisies. From the distance there is the sound of a cowbell; over the mountain a plane flies purposefully toward the city. There is a faraway sound of hay baling in the North Field. After tea, everyone takes a basket to gather fresh petals from the garden for making potpourri.

GARDEN TEA PARTY

Minted Iced Tea

Fresh Berries with sugar   Bread-and-Butter Sandwiches

"Plain Cake" ringed with field daisies

Crisp Thin Brownies

Herb Cookies

MINTED ICED TEA

5 tsp. (or teabags) of tea	1 cup sugar
1 lemon	1 lime
3 or 4 sprigs fresh mint	2 qts. boiling water

Put dry tea and sugar into a deep bowl. Cut lemon and lime into quarters. Squeeze juice from the quarters into bowl with fingers, then drop in the chunks. Add the mint and mash with a spurtle (see Glossary). Pour boiling water over this mixture. "It looks funny but don't worry," warns *The Buttery Book.* Cover and let stand 4 minutes. Strain into a pitcher and cool. Serve in tall glasses with ice. This makes about eight servings.

BREAD-AND-BUTTER SANDWICHES

Making paper-thin sandwiches is easier if the bread is buttered before it is cut from the loaf. To do this, cut the heel off the loaf. With softened butter, spread the end of the loaf, then carefully cut the slice off thin. Repeat for half the loaf. Cut the other half without buttering and then put together one for one with a buttered piece.

Or spread half the loaf with butter as above, cutting the slices a little thicker. Spread the other half with mayonnaise. Score with a fork a fresh, washed, crisp-cold cucumber or radishes; slice thin. Put the slices on the buttered bread, touch lightly with salt, put a mayonnaise-bread slice on top. Trim crusts and edges; cut to pretty shapes. Serve on a glass plate. Watercress, nasturtium leaves, minced parsley, and chopped green peppers are also delicious for garden tea sandwiches.

"PLAIN CAKE"

"Plain Cake" is not really so very plain, but it's our familiar name for a rich tea cake with no icing, just a dusting of powdered sugar. Our receipt is a small version of Almond Pound Cake, just right for company tea.

Grease well and dust with flour a small (about 8-by-2½-inch) pottery Turk's head mold, or use one 8-inch layer-cake pan.

With a wire whisk beat 3 egg yolks until light. Gradually add ¾ cup sugar (reserve 2 Tbs.) and beat until light. Add ⅓ cup good brandy or cognac and ¼ tsp. almond extract. With a wooden spoon lightly beat into this mixture ¾ cup sifted cake flour. Add ¾ cup finely ground blanched almonds. Stir in lightly ¼ lb. melted and cooled butter.

Beat 3 egg whites and ⅛ tsp. salt together until soft peaks form. Add to the egg whites the reserved 2 Tbs. sugar and beat until stiff.

Lightly fold egg whites into cake mixture. Turn into mold and bake in a moderate oven (350°) about 30 minutes, until golden brown and the top springs back when touched with finger. Cool 10 to 15 minutes. Run a knife around the edge to loosen, turn out onto wire rack right-side-up until cold. With a flour sifter, dust with powdered sugar. Put the cake on a pretty plate, ring the base with daisies or honeysuckle or sweet peas. Cut into thin slices for serving.

CRISP THIN BROWNIES

1 cup butter	1 cup cake flour
4 squares melted chocolate	4 tsp. vanilla
4 eggs	½ tsp. salt
2 cups sugar	

Melt chocolate and butter together. Beat eggs, add sugar and vanilla, add melted chocolate and butter. Mix in flour and salt. Bake in two 10-by-10-inch shallow pans for 35 minutes in a slow oven (325°). When cool, cut in small squares.

HERB COOKIES

Cream together 1 cup softened butter and 2 cups sugar. Add 4 eggs one at a time; beat well to blend after each addition. Sift together in a separate bowl 4 cups flour, ½ tsp. soda, 2 tsp. baking powder, and ½ tsp. salt. Add any one of the following: 2 Tbs. caraway seeds; crushed coriander or cardamom seeds; or crushed dried marjoram leaves. Fold herbs into dry ingredients.

With wooden spoon, stir dry ingredients into creamed mixture until well mixed. Form into several balls and chill. Roll each ball one at a time about ⅛ inch thick and cut with small round cooky cutter. Bake on greased cooky sheet for about 10 minutes, until lightly browned, in a moderately hot oven (375°).

POTPOURRI

Gather petals of fully opened flowers before they begin to fade. Use plenty of rose petals in pink, red, yellow, copper. Add delphinium florets and phlox; pansy, Johnny-jump-up, viola, lavender, heliotrope; and any of the herb flowers except those of the onion family.

Dry them as they are gathered on paper-towel-covered trays or on sheets of newspaper in a warm, dry, shady place. Keep them dry in a basket until the garden ceases to bloom and gathering has ended, then spill into a large bowl. Add powdered clove, cinnamon, and nutmeg, about a teaspoonful in all to a quart of flowers. Add dried grated lemon or orange peel. Do not put in orris root (some people get hay fever from it). Toss all together like a big colorful salad, and put into old ginger jars, old sugar bowls, apothecary jars, or any pretty glass or china bits with lids which may be available. Tie with a ribbon bow and put in the Christmas-present chest for favorite garden friends.

In the winter, tea is served in the best parlor with the warmth of a hearth-fire to take the chill off the leafless look of the garden and the sleet singing against the windowpanes. Favorite friends come in for visits and so the Canton cups are taken from the shelf, and the spirit lamp is lighted under the silver teakettle. A lemon and an orange are sliced thinly. The ceremony of afternoon tea is a gracious one, long remembered by the guests. We make sure the cups and the silver are sparkling clean, the candles fresh and new. The best tea napkins are used, such fun to iron to glossy smoothness. Heirloom silver teaspoons with the funny rounded bowls are better for sipping. Water is fresh-drawn and boiling. Sometimes the tea is our favorite Oolong, sometimes it will be a smoky or a spicy one, always carefully measured a teaspoon per cup of water and one extra for the pot.

Tiny sweet scones are spread with thick country cream, a spoonful of jam, or flower-garden honey atop. Pass a generous plate of coconut squares and pineapple drops, and the delicious Charlotte's Cake. Here in our favorite chairs with a warm hooked rug under our feet and ancestors looking down upon us from frames on the wall, we savor the tea and the moments. Draw the curtains against the darkening winter afternoon, light the candles, and enjoy the comfort and companionship of tea in the best parlor.

WINTER TEA PARTY

Sweet Scones   *Thick Country Cream*

Best Jam   *Flower-Garden Honey*

Coconut Squares   *Pineapple Drops*

Charlotte's Cake

Tea

Reminiscent of Devonshire cottage teas, or of Grandmother pouring at the best-parlor tea table in rustling black silk are sweet scones with "clotted cream," which can be made at home from scalded whole rich Jersey milk. If one doesn't have such, a combination of 1 quart milk (not homogenized) and 1 pint heavy cream will work quite well.

Put the milk–cream in a flat pan or milk dish on the lowest possible heat or in a pan of hot water for 4 or 5 hours. When the cream on the surface appears yellow, wrinkled, and leathery, remove from the heat and, without disturbing the cream, cool overnight in the butt'ry (or in the ice-box). Next morning, skim cream off with a perforated spoon or cream skimmer. Stir a very little to smoothen with a fork. Serve in a dish with a spoon, spread on a scone, add a whole strawberry or a dip of best jam or a generous dribble of honey—and forget the calories.

SWEET SCONES

Sift together 2 cups sifted flour, 1 tsp. salt, 4 Tbs. sugar, and 1 Tbs. baking powder. With pastry blender cut in 3 Tbs. butter.

Beat well 2 egg yolks and add to them ⅓ cup heavy cream. Stir egg mixture and flour mixture together into a soft dough. Turn out on floured pastry board and knead about 20 times. Roll out about ½ inch thick and cut with small round cooky cutter. Place on ungreased cooky sheet. Brush tops with egg white or milk and sprinkle with a mixture of 2 Tbs. sugar and ½ tsp. cinnamon. Bake in a hot oven (450°) until lightly browned.

COCONUT SQUARES

Mix well together:	½ cup firm brown sugar
1 cup sifted flour	½ cup softened butter

Press firmly with hand into bottom of an ungreased 11-by-7-inch cake pan and bake in moderate oven (350°) for 10 minutes. Remove from oven and spread with the following:

Mix together:	1 cup brown sugar
2 well-beaten eggs	1 tsp. vanilla

Sift together and add:	1 tsp. baking powder
2 Tbs. flour	½ tsp. salt

Add a generous cup of shredded coconut and 1 cup chopped walnuts or almonds or pecans. Bake an additional 20 to 25 minutes, until lightly browned. Cut in squares or bars when cool.

PINEAPPLE DROPS

Cream together ½ cup butter and 1 cup brown sugar.

Add:	½ tsp. salt
1 well-beaten egg	½ cup drained crushed pineapple
1 tsp. vanilla	½ cup finely chopped nuts

Sift together, then add:	2 cups sifted flour
1 tsp. baking powder	½ tsp. soda

Drop by teaspoonfuls on a cooky sheet and bake in a hot oven (400°) until lightly browned.

CHARLOTTE'S CAKE

The men and boys in the family relish Charlotte's Cake especially. It is an old-fashioned and delicious cake.

Mix together: ¾ cup good corn oil
2 cups sugar   1 egg

Beat well. Sift together three times:

4 level tsp. soda   ⅔ cup cocoa
2½ cups flour   ¾ tsp. salt

Add dry ingredients to sugar mixture alternately with 2 cups buttermilk. Bake in a moderate oven (350°) about half an hour in greased and floured baking pans.

FROSTING

Mix together: 1 Tbs. vanilla
¼ lb. soft butter   Pinch of salt
About 2 lbs. powdered sugar   Enough cream for spreading easily

To serve, put on an old-fashioned cake plate, with a silver knife and tea plates beside it for helping one's self.

NEW YEAR'S DAY OPEN HOUSE

VALENTINE'S DAY

EASTER BREAKFAST

MAY BASKET DAY

AFTERNOON TEA PARTIES

WEDDING RECEPTION

WEDDING ANNIVERSARY DINNER FOR TWO

PICNIC BY THE RIVER

Wedding Reception

ON a June day fair and blue of sky, the white-spired village church has opened wide its doors and every pew is filled with neighbors, friends, and relatives. Tapering white candles light the dimness. White old-fashioned roses and delphinium from the garden and ribbons along the aisles of white-painted pews decorate in welcome of a pretty young bride in her mother's ivory-silk wedding gown, who walks in radiance from the altar with her happy husband.

The old house is filled with flowers, too, and once again the best parlor is alight, with golden sunshine streaming through open small-paned windows. Champagne Punch is in a bowl at one end of the table; at the other end coffee is served from Grandmother Thompson's silver coffee urn. Petits Fours, tiny heart-shaped Sugar Cookies, bite-size Jam Tarts, Watercress Rolled Sandwiches, and Checkerboard Chicken Sandwiches fill silver trays on the snowy tablecloth.

The Wedding Cake is made according to one of our most treasured family receipts, used since Great-Great-Grandmother was a bride in England. Six alternating layers of white cake "for the bride" and dark cake "for the groom," it was made in the butt'ry weeks ago to await its frosting of white and its decorating in loops and festoons of icing. A bouquet fashioned of sugared rose petals adorns the top.

Uncle Doug toasts the bride in champagne punch, then in a time-honored tradition throws his glass to smash into the fireplace that it may never be used for any other purpose than this forever toast. Catch the bride's bouquet of sweet peas, baby's-breath, and rosebuds from the garden and grab a handful of rose petals from a basket to throw as she disappears in a cloud of dust down the shaded country road. Then wedding guests linger in the garden, children romp in the barn and never mind the best clothes. There is plenty of neighborly help for bringing order again to the house.

THE WEDDING COLLATION

Champagne Punch

Watercress Rolled Sandwiches   *Checkerboard Chicken Sandwiches*

Petits Fours   *Heart-shaped Sugar Cookies*

Tiny Jam Tarts

Wedding Cake

CHAMPAGNE PUNCH

A day or so before the reception, mix well in a gallon covered crock and chill:

2 cups good brandy
2 bottles good sauterne
1 to 1½ cups sugar, mixed in well until dissolved
Unpeeled thin slices of 6 oranges and 6 lemons

Just before serving the champagne, strain this mixture into a large glass bowl and rest it on ice in a larger silver bowl. In this way the punch is not diluted by melting ice. Add to the mixture 2 quarts chilled ginger ale, 6 bottles chilled champagne, and some fresh mint leaves. Add a pint of fresh small strawberries, wild if there are a-plenty in the old orchard.

In each punch cup, place a small cube of pineapple, fresh or canned, and serve the punch with a glass or silver ladle. This serves about thirty guests generously.

WATERCRESS ROLLED SANDWICHES

Soften a pound of cream cheese and thin slightly with sweet cream. With a sharp knife or scissors, cut finely three bunches of fresh watercress. Mix the watercress and cream cheese together.

Soften a pound of butter. Remove the crusts from two sandwich loaves each of white and whole-wheat bread. Spread butter on the end and cut a thin slice. Spread this with the chopped watercress and roll firmly, holding with a toothpick if necessary. Put in a long cake pan, cover with slightly dampened paper toweling and a clean dishtowel. Chill well. Arrange on doily on a platter or silver or glass tray; garnish with extra sprigs of water-cress.

CHECKERBOARD CHICKEN SANDWICHES

Remove all crusts from unsliced sandwich loaves, white and whole wheat. Unsliced bread may have to be ordered in advance from the bakery.

Cut six uniform slices lengthwise of each loaf, about half an inch thick, a total of twelve slices. Put four long slices together in this way, alternating white, whole wheat, white, whole wheat: butter a slice of whole wheat and spread thinly with chicken filling; place on top of it a slice of white, and butter and spread thinly with chicken filling; repeat with another slice of whole wheat. Now add a slice of white unbuttered. Do this three times, to make three stacks of four slices each.

Now cut each stack from the top six times in lengthwise slices. Butter the new slices and spread thinly with chicken as before, putting four slices together and alternating white and whole wheat colors. You will have two slices left over: cut in half and stack one-half on top of the other. You will have 4½ loaves. Trim them carefully. The end of each loaf will show the checkerboard pattern.

Wrap in wax paper the loaves thus made. Put in a pan with damp paper towels and a clean dishtowel over, and chill thoroughly. When ready to serve, slice crosswise one-half inch thick.

Chicken filling is made by putting through meat grinder, using finest blade, 8 cups of cooked chicken and 4 cups of celery. Add to this and mix well ¼ cup lemon juice, 2 tsp. salt, ½ tsp. pepper, and 2 cups mayonnaise.

This checkerboard sandwich is handsome and delicious just buttered, without the chicken filling, especially for afternoon tea.

PETITS FOURS

Butter and line with paper, a 13-by-9-by-2-inch pan. Heat oven to moderate (350°).

Cream together ¼ cup butter and ¼ cup other fine shortening. Add and cream until light 1 cup sugar, ½ tsp. vanilla, and ½ tsp. almond extract.

Sift together 2 cups sifted cake flour, 3 tsp. baking powder, and ¼ tsp. salt.

Beat the dry mixture into the creamed mixture alternately with ¾ cup rich milk. Beat 6 egg whites until foamy, gradually add ¼ cup sugar and beat to soft peaks. Fold egg whites into cake mixture.

Bake about 40 minutes, or until cake springs back when lightly touched with finger in the center. Cool 10 minutes and put on a cake rack. When thoroughly cool, trim off the crusty sides. Cut into small cubes, rounds, and diamonds about 1½ or 2 inches.

Arrange pieces on cake racks over cooky sheets (to catch icing drips) and pour icing over the cakes, being careful to coat each piece well. This receipt makes about 54 small cakes. Double receipt and bake in two pans for about 100 cakes.

PETITS FOURS ICING

Cook together to thin-syrup stage (226°):

3 cups sugar   1½ cups water
¼ tsp. cream of tartar

Remove from fire and cool to lukewarm. Add 1 tsp. vanilla. Beat in about 2½ cups powdered sugar until of pouring consistency but not too thin.

Decorate the cakes after icing hardens with frosting forced through a decorating tube or with sugared petals or flowers. If using frosting, mix together 2 Tbs. soft butter, 2½ cups sifted powdered sugar and sweet cream to smoothen. Add one unbeaten egg white, ½ tsp. vanilla, and ⅛ tsp. cream of tartar. A little more sweet cream may be added if needed. Divide into small bowls, color with pink, green, and yellow food coloring to pastel shades.

TINY JAM TARTS

Make a receipt of Rich Pastry. Sift together into a bowl 3 cups sifted flour, ½ tsp. salt, ½ tsp. baking powder. Cut in with pastry blender 1 cup shortening (good lard) and ½ cup butter. With a fork beat one egg well, add to the first mixture together with about 5 Tbs. ice water. Mix all together lightly with a fork as quickly as possible; roll into a ball. Chill at least two hours, overnight if possible.

Roll out thinly on a floured board. Cut out rounds with a small (about 2-inch diameter) cooky cutter. Flute edges with fingers and tuck into small (1½-inch) muffin tins. Prick each one in two directions with a fork. Bake in a hot oven (400°) until lightly brown. Remove from baking tins.

Just before serving, fill each tart with a teaspoonful of firm strawberry, raspberry, or other jam or jelly. Top with a little dab of sweetened whipped cream and arrange on a doily-covered silver tray.

Wedding Cake

Two people working at once will speed the making of this old-fashioned wedding cake.

THE BRIDE'S CAKE

Whites of 6 eggs
1 cup sugar
½ cup butter
½ cup sweet cream
2½ cups flour
1 Tbs. baking powder

1 lb. chopped almonds
½ lb chopped citron
½ lb. grated coconut
1 tsp. rose water
1 tsp. lemon extract

Cream together the butter and sugar; add the cream. Sift together the sifted flour and baking powder and add to creamed mixture. Add flavorings, then mix in the chopped fruit and nuts. Beat the egg whites until stiff and fold into cake batter.

THE GROOM'S CAKE

1 cup sugar
½ cup brown sugar
1 cup butter
Yolks of 6 eggs
2 cups flour
1½ lbs. seeded (not seedless) raisins

1 lb. dried currants
½ lb. chopped citron
¼ lb. chopped nuts
⅔ cup good whiskey
1 tsp. soda
½ tsp. each of ground cloves, cinnamon, nutmeg, allspice

Cream sugar and butter until light; add eggs and beat well. Add flour, fruit, whiskey, soda, and spices and mix together.

For each cake, butter well and flour three pans, 12 inches, 9 inches, and 6 inches in diameter. Bake in a slow oven (300°) for 2½ hours or a little more. When done, remove from oven, cool for 10 minutes, then put on cake racks to cool completely. May be stored for several days wrapped separately in foil. When ready to frost, put together in alternate graduated layers with Wedding Cake Icing.

WEDDING CAKE ICING

1 cup soft butter	8 to 10 egg whites
6 lbs. sifted powdered sugar	½ cup sweet cream (not heavy)
1 tsp. salt	3 tsp. vanilla

In a large bowl, cream and beat butter until light. Gradually add the sugar and egg whites alternately and beat well. Add salt and vanilla and mix in well. Add enough cream to make a good spreading consistency. Wedding Cake Icing should not be tinted.

Cover a round piece of white cardboard with a lace-paper doily. Place the 12-inch Bride's Cake on this; frost thinly, then place the 12-inch Groom's Cake on top. Cut a 9-inch round of white cardboard and center on the lower cake. Place the 9-inch Bride's Cake on the cardboard, frost thinly, and then place the 9-inch Groom's Cake on top. Do the same with the two 6-inch layers, then frost the whole cake. While frosting the cake, protect the doily with a strip of wax paper; remove the paper when frosted. Keep the frosting bowl covered with a damp cloth while working so the frosting will remain moist.

For decorating the cake, use a decorating tube or cornucopia. Be lavish with loops, festoons, and rosettes of the icing on the sides. Crystallize whole single white roses or individual rose petals and leaves and fashion into a bouquet for the top of the cake.

Wedding Anniversary Dinner for Two

WEDDING anniversaries are special for just two people really, and so for many years has this day of quiet joy been celebrated with our Anniversary Dinner for Two. Mother and Father on their anniversary used to take the train to the city, where they spent several days away from family and farm and business cares, living in luxury in the elegance of their favorite hotel. Their anniversary dinner was invariably based on champagne and filet mignon—and it's our favorite, too. Grandmother and Grandfather with eleven children were "alone" in the midst of their family on anniversary day, no less a twosome in spite of the throng.

We set the Queen Anne table with finest wedding-present linen, china, crystal, and silver before the hearth in the best parlor. Sweetheart roses are arranged in a little silver basket. Champagne is chilling in the cold-beaded brass champagne bucket with pewter handles we two once carried with glee from an antique shop. Slide the dessert into the oven and time it carefully so that it will be puffy and brown and just done by dessert time. Keep the dinner hot on its platter in the old toleware tin warming oven on the hearth. Keep the green salad crispy cold in the ice-box to be tossed at table as a separate course. Light the candles to gleam on mantle and table. Then pour champagne into two sparkling Waterford crystal glasses bought on our wedding trip for just this yearly celebrating. We serve the dinner to ourselves and there is no hurry, plenty of time for talk, for remembering, for planning great things ahead.

ANNIVERSARY DINNER

Champagne   *Cheese Crisps*

Filet Mignon broiled   *Hearth-baked Potato with*

on the Hearth   *plenty of butter*

Beach Plum Jelly

Asparagus Spears with Hollandaise Sauce

Green Salad with Roquefort in Cut-glass Bowl

Grand Marnier Soufflé

Mocha-Java in Canton after-dinner cups with Whipped Cream and Nutmeg

CHEESE CRISPS

Dough for these crisp wafers is kept rolled and chilled in the ice-box for serving with cocktails, morning coffee for callers, or with a luncheon salad. They are sliced thin and served hot from the oven.

Grate 1 lb. aged cheese (sharp American or Cheddar, not the gluey kind). Pour over the cheese one-half cup of melted butter.

Sift together 2 cups flour, 1½ tsp. salt, and ¼ tsp. red pepper. Add this to cheese, working ingredients with fingers until well mixed. Press with hands into two long rolls. Wrap with wax paper and chill. Cut in very thin slices, put on greased cooky sheet, and bake in a hot (450°) oven about 7 minutes or until lightly browned. Do not overbrown. Serve hot.

This dough will keep for weeks in the ice-box and may be sliced as needed. Mostly it disappears fast.

FILET MIGNON BROILED ON THE HEARTH

Have the family butcher cut 1½ or 2 inches thick his finest beef tenderloin, one tenderloin slice per person. Shape it neatly into a round pat of meat, but don't mash it.

Grease well a small wrought-iron hearth broiler. Have ready a flat area of red coals, put broiler over it and quickbrown the tenderloins, five to seven minutes on each side. Salt, and fresh-grind the pepper, and remove the tenderloins to a small heated platter. Put a little piece of butter on each tenderloin. Keep hot on a trivet near the coals or in a warming oven. Garnish with parsley.

BAKED POTATO

Choose carefully, scrub and rub with butter one good-sized baking potato for each person. Roll in foil and twist ends of foil to seal. Put close to or even in the coals of the fire and turn occasionally. Bake until done (about an hour, depending on the size). Test with two-tined fork. Remove from fire and foil, split the top with a sharp knife and squeeze the potato to break it. Add salt, freshly ground pepper, a generous piece of butter, and a little chopped parsley or chives. Serve with extra butter, sour cream, or rich sweet cream.

BEACH PLUM JELLY

An old New England favorite, this jelly is tart and is best served with meats and game. Gather the beach plums from the bushes when they are not too ripe—still reddish in color. Stem and wash them and put in a large kettle.

Pour in cold water to a little over half. Cook until plums are soft. Strain through jelly bag all night.

In the morning, measure the strained juice. Measure in another dish an equal amount of sugar. Bring juice to the boiling point and boil hard for five minutes. Add sugar and stir until well dissolved.

Continue easy boiling and after about five minutes begin to test by dipping a spoon into the jelly. Let it cool a little, then turn spoon on its side and drip the jelly into the kettle. It is done when it "sheets," or two drops fall as one drop (220°). Pour into hot glasses, seal with paraffin, and cover.

ASPARAGUS SPEARS WITH HOLLANDAISE SAUCE

Stand freshly gathered asparagus, tied together in a bundle, in the bottom of a double boiler in one-half cup of boiling water. Turn the top of boiler upside down over spears to cover. Cook until the large ends are tender, usually about ten or twelve minutes. Drain and salt. Arrange in a hot dish (do not use silver, for the Hollandaise may blacken it). Pour over it a generous amount of Hollandaise; dust with paprika.

HOLLANDAISE SAUCE

This may be made ahead of time and rewarmed in a jar set in a pan of warm (not hot) water.

In the top of a double boiler beat well with a fork 2 egg yolks. Add the juice of one large lemon (most people don't put in enough lemon) and mix well. Cut ¼ lb. of butter in about six pieces. Spear one at a time with fork and stir into lemon mixture until melted. Hold the pan over, not in, the boiling water and don't be in a hurry to cook it too fast or it will curdle. It takes only a few minutes anyway. Season with salt, white pepper, and a couple of drops of Tabasco sauce.

GREEN SALAD

There is no receipt in the *Buttery Books* for making a green salad. Like almost any good dish, green salad is best when mixed with imagination and served with a little drama. Salad should be its own course and practice makes perfect.

Rub well a sparkling glass bowl (or a wooden bowl) with the cut halves of a garlic bud. With your hands, tear into the bowl fresh, clean, crisp but dry lettuce into pieces of a size to eat. Add other greens if you like. We like best garden lettuce with one finely torn leaf of lovage or celery, a little parsley; we don't use tough greens. Add a slice or two of onion or tomato wedges or carrot if you like. Some cubes of avocado are delicious added at the last.

Keep the ingredients refrigerated in the bowl and bring to the table at the last possible moment, with vinegar and oil in cruets. Mix at table. Do it with flourish.

Into a salad-serving spoon, pour olive oil and distribute over the greens, about one spoonful per person. Mix gently until greens are well coated. Into the spoon now put about a half-teaspoonful of salt per person (or to your taste), then grind a dusting of pepper over this. Over the salt and pepper in the spoon, pour a good wine or tarragon or cider vinegar and mix together well with serving fork. Distribute over the greens. A good proportion of vinegar to oil is about one vinegar to two oil. Mix gently and well. Over the top crumble small pieces of Roquefort and turn over the salad once again.

GRAND MARNIER SOUFFLÉ

Make a thick white sauce of 3 Tbs. butter, 3 Tbs. flour, and one cup milk. When thick, remove from fire. Add 3 well-beaten egg yolks and one-half cup of sugar and stir well. Add 3 Tbs. Grand Marnier.

Butter well and dust with sugar the inside of a quart-and-a-half straight-sided soufflé dish.

Beat 4 egg whites until they are stiff; fold into the mixture. Turn into the soufflé dish and bake in a moderate oven (350°) until puffed and nicely browned, about 45 to 50 minutes in all. If it browns too quickly, turn oven down (to 325°). If you wish a tall soufflé, use a quart dish and fasten a doubled strip of foil around the edge of the dish to be about 3 inches higher than the dish. Remove this strip carefully before serving. Bring to table for serving *immediately*, to insure a high handsome soufflé.

This delicate soufflé needs no sauce, although a spoonful of tutti-frutti may be spooned on if desired.

Mocha-Java coffee can be bought already mixed and ground from S. S. Pierce. It comes in their familiar red tin. Percolate it or drip it as you do regular coffee. We use it extra strong for after dinner, add a spoonful of sweetened whipped cream, and grate nutmeg over it.

Picnic by the River

WHEN city cousins come to visit, there is never any wondering how to entertain them. Picnic by the River is one of the happiest activities of country living. Sometimes it is the annual Sunday school picnic held on the riverbank; preparations at home are the same. There are sack races and one-legged races and egg races in the morning; while the ladies set the long picnic tables, the grandfathers play horseshoes and the fathers join their sons in a baseball game. But the most fun of all is our own picnic when company comes.

The butt'ry is buzzing with mixing of something. Everybody has an assigned job. Someone gets all the picnic baskets down from the attic and passes them around to be filled. One basket holds bathing suits and towels, a bar or two of soap, combs and brushes for doing wet hair. One is packed with the old red tablecloth, a red napkin wrapped around a fork and spoons for each of us, big blue granite cups and plates, a half-dozen serving spoons.

The ice cream is frozen and has been packed in salt and ice. Graham bread was made yesterday, the better for sandwiches today, spread with yellow homemade butter. Potato salad, too, was made and put in the ice-box to chill overnight for better flavor. Brownies, freshly made and cut in the pan, are thick and chewy and the heavenly smell of chocolate fills the kitchen. Yesterday the chickens were caught and dressed for frying early this morning and they cool in the butt'ry, then are packed in their own basket. There are pickles and deviled (stuffed) eggs; a gallon jug of icy lemonade with floating slices of lemon and mint for garnish.

It used to be that all the baskets and the tub of ice cream were packed into the farm wagon for driving to the river. Now the station wagon is loaded and we are off via the woods road to the covered bridge. The river comes from the mountaintop and tumbles over boulders until, just around the bend above the bridge, it suddenly slows. Here at the foot of the woods, the river is tame and quiet and shallow enough for children to play in; there is a deep pool for swimming under the opposite bank. Everyone jumps in for splashing and even the corgi gets a frolicsome bath.

Baskets are soon unpacked and such quantities of food disappear there is nothing to take home except empty baskets. So fill them with pine cones and ferns and wild berries and flowers. Rinse the dishes in the river, pack the wagon. Then sit in a circle and sing old ballads until sundown. It's time to go home for doing chores, and what a night for sound sleeping this will be!

PICNIC DINNER

Crisp Fried Chicken   Potato Salad

Stuffed Eggs   Pickles   Graham Bread Sandwiches

Vanilla Custard Ice Cream or Lemon Crunch Ice Cream

Chewy Brownies   Lots of Lemonade

CRISP FRIED CHICKEN

Cut into serving pieces two or three 3-to-4-lb. fryers. Be sure to cut the wishbone piece off before splitting the breast. In a bowl put one cup of flour, 2 tsp. salt, ½ tsp. freshly ground pepper, ½ tsp. crushed rosemary. Dip each piece of chicken into this and spoon flour over, being sure to cover thoroughly. Brown on all sides in butter and other good shortening, about half and half, a half-inch deep in a heavy iron skillet. Turn with tongs while browning.

When well browned, cover and cook over low heat until tender, 30 to 40 minutes. Uncover and cook an additional 10 minutes to crisp. When cool, pack in a basket lined with a napkin and foil. Cover loosely until served.

POTATO SALAD

First make the dressing. In top of a double boiler, beat well with a wire whisk 2 egg yolks. Add 2 tsp. each of sugar, Colman's dry mustard, melted butter, 2 Tbs. flour. Add 6 Tbs. rich milk. Cook and stir while adding slowly 6 Tbs. good cider vinegar. Continue cooking and stirring until thick. Cool. Store dressing in the ice-box and always mix with an equal part of sour cream or heavy sweet cream.

Boil until tender but not too soft one firm, unpeeled potato for each serving. When just cool enough to handle, peel off jackets and slice potatoes into a large bowl. Add 1 tsp. salt, ¼ tsp. freshly ground pepper, 2 Tbs. grated or chopped onion, 2 or 3 hard-cooked eggs cut into pieces. Mix well but gently; fold in dressing mixed with sour cream.

Put salad into a yellow bowl with brown stripes (it tastes better). Smooth the top a little and garnish with chopped chives, sliced hard-cooked egg, and a sprig of parsley. Cool in ice-box, overnight if possible, for best flavor.

If there isn't time to make boiled dressing, add sour cream and a little Colman's dry mustard to boughten mayonnaise. The result isn't as good, but it will do in a pinch.

STUFFED EGGS

Be sure to use fine, fresh eggs. Hard-cook them and pour cold water over them. Peel and cut eggs in half lengthwise. Mash yolk in a small bowl and add, for each egg: dash of salt and pepper, about ½ tsp. oil-and-vinegar dressing, 1 tsp. mayonnaise. Fill each half of the cooked whites with this mixture; pile loosely. Decorate with a few sprigs of thyme and chervil.

MOTHER'S CUCUMBER PICKLES

Slice large (firm and not seedy) cucumbers lengthwise, and let them stand in ice water three hours. In the bottom of a quart jar, place one small sliced onion and one slice each of red and green pepper. Lay the slices of cucumber in upright, and to every four or five put in one piece of thin-sliced celery. Prepare the following syrup and when boiling pour into the jar to the top: one quart vinegar, one cup sugar and one-half cup salt. Add one Tbs. mixed pickling spices. Seal the jars while mixture is hot and let stand several weeks before using.

This makes nice crisp tart pickles and it is very little trouble.

GRAHAM BREAD

This receipt makes 2 large or 6 tiny loaves.

Soften 1 package dry yeast in ¼ cup warm water. In a large bowl combine ½ cup firmly packed brown sugar, 3 Tbs. butter, 1 Tbs. salt, and 1 cup boiling water. Add ¾ cup cold water. Cool mixture to lukewarm and stir in the yeast.

Add gradually 4 cups graham flour, ½ cup wheat germ, and 1 to 1½ cups white flour to make a stiff dough. Knead on a lightly floured board until smooth and satiny and no longer sticky, perhaps 10 minutes. Place in a greased bowl and cover with a clean dishtowel. Let rise in a warm place about 2 hours, until double.

Punch down, let rise another 30 minutes. Then divide dough into parts for loaves (2 large or 6 tiny loaves). Shape nicely, folding ends under firmly, and put into buttered pans. Cover with clean dishtowel again. Let rise until double.

Bake in a moderate oven (350°) for 50 to 60 minutes, or until the loaves "thump" hollow and done. (It takes less time for the tiny loaves— 30 to 40 minutes.) Remove from pans immediately. Brush tops with butter.

VANILLA CUSTARD ICE CREAM

Combine in a saucepan 2¼ cups sugar, 6 Tbs. flour, and ½ tsp. salt. Stir in slowly 5 cups scalded rich milk and cook until thickened. Remove from fire for a moment and add slowly while stirring 6 beaten egg yolks. Return to the fire and cook over low heat for several minutes longer. Chill well in the ice-box. Pour into a gallon freezer can, add 4 cups heavy cream and 3 Tbs. vanilla. Freeze and pack.

LEMON CRUNCH ICE CREAM

In a large saucepan, scald 5 cups rich milk. Add 2¼ cups sugar and stir until well dissolved. Add slowly the beaten yolks of 2 eggs; stir and cook for 2 minutes. Remove from the fire and cool thoroughly. Add 3 cups heavy cream, the grated peel of 3 lemons, and ⅔ cup fresh lemon juice. Fold in the stiffly beaten whites of 2 eggs and turn the mixture into a gallon freezer can. Turn for 10 minutes or so, and when the mixture begins to pull a little, open freezer, stir in quickly 1 cup of lemon drops which have been crushed with a hammer in a cloth bag. Complete the freezing. Delectable.

CHEWY BROWNIES

Melt together 4 squares chocolate and ½ cup butter, then cool. In a large bowl, beat until light 4 eggs. Add ¼ tsp. salt. Gradually add 2 cups sugar and beat the mixture until light and creamy. Fold in the chocolate mixture. Add 2 tsp. vanilla. Add 1 cup sifted flour and beat until smooth and light.

Fold in 1 cup chopped butternuts or black walnuts. Pour the mixture into a generously buttered and floured 13-by-9-inch pan and bake the brownies in a rather slow oven (325°) for about 25 or 30 minutes. Do not overbake.

Remove from the oven and put on the top of the brownies about ⅔ of a 6½-oz. package of peppermint-flavored chocolate patties. Return to oven with door open until topping is just soft. With a small spatula, spread the frosting. When quite cool, cut the brownies into large squares. Take to the picnic in the pan.

LEMONADE

Roll 12 lemons to soften, then squeeze juice. Add 1¼ cups sugar and stir well. Add 3 quarts water. Taste for sweetness, adding more sugar if necessary. Chill.

Pour into picnic thermos jug and add ice to fill, also several lemon slices, 2 or 3 mint sprigs. This receipt makes 16 generous helpings, can easily be doubled.

Breakfast Under the Apple Tree

THE morning we're sure the black flies have gone for the summer, we have breakfast under the apple tree and each day the sun shines finds us there for our first meal of the day until frosty mornings come. Dan Mahoney, the blacksmith, made the square wrought-iron marble-topped table for us, just the right size to fit under arching branches laden in spring with pink blossoms, in summer with dark green leaves, in fall with red crab-apples. A robin builds her nest high in the top of the tree. We watch the humming-birds sipping the petunias, columbine, and sweet William in the border nearby as we sip until the last drop of coffee in the pot is gone.

The fruit course is whatever is in season, from rhubarb and strawberries right through to applesauce. Usually we serve the fruit with sugar and plenty of thick fresh cream. In September we even peel and slice fresh pears into a bowl to be served with sugar and cream, delicate and delicious.

Our favorite breakfast under the apple tree is eggs coddled in a little cup, hot gems with a plate of freshly molded butter, plenty of coffee. We have several kinds of good muffins, always made in the iron gem pans— spice, blueberry, date-nut, orange marmalade. Sometimes we make a quick coffee cake or wrap a stack of hot buttered or cinnamon toast in a linen napkin to keep warm while we eat our fruit.

Everything, including dishes, fits onto one large tray that is loaded in the kitchen. When the gems are taken out of the oven and popped into their basket, everything else is ready, too, and is carried out to the apple tree. It's always a simple breakfast, plenty of it, easy to serve. And it's a lazy breakfast as we dawdle over the good eating, the delicious coffee and the sights, sounds, and heavenly fragrance of the dewy garden in early morning.

BREAKFAST OUT-OF-DOORS

Fresh Fruit in Season
Fresh Jumbo Eggs Coddled in a Cup
Hot Gems or
Jiffy Coffee Cake
Coffee

FRESH JUMBO EGGS CODDLED IN A CUP

Into a saucepan pour a cupful of water and put on the stove to boil. Place a pottery cup of small size on the bottom of the saucepan for each serving of egg. Into each cup put a piece of butter the size of a thimble. Then into each cup carefully break a fresh jumbo egg (if it's double-yolked, so much the better). Cover the pan and cook until the white is set and no longer jiggly. Salt and freshly ground pepper are added at the table, to taste.

HOT GEMS

In a clean gallon glass jar with a snug-fitting cover, we keep a supply of muffin mix which we make at a fraction of the cost of prepared mixes. It's handy on a shelf of the butt'ry, can be dipped into in a second, and the gems are in the oven in a trice. It makes in all about 12 dozen gems. Depending on appetites, it keeps without refrigeration for several weeks, or can be kept in the ice-box.

5 lbs flour	3 Tbs. salt
Generous ½ (about ⅔) cup baking powder	1¾ lbs. butter
	1 Tbs. mace

Mix dry ingredients together in a large dishpan. Cut in butter with pastry blender until finely divided (coarse meal consistency). Put into a large glass jar and cover tightly.

To make *biscuits* from this mix, measure 4 cups of mix into a bowl. Add a cup of rich milk and stir until a soft dough is formed. Knead on lightly floured board about 10 times. Pat or roll ½ inch thick. Cut with floured cutter. Bake on ungreased baking sheet in a hot oven (450°) for 12 to 15 minutes until browned.

For *plain muffins*, measure 4 cups of the mix into a bowl. Add ¼ cup sugar, 2 well-beaten eggs, and 1½ cups rich milk. Add a tablespoon of sour cream for extra goodness. Mix until dry ingredients are dampened. Spoon into buttered gem pans and bake in a hot oven (425°) about 20 minutes. This will make 2 dozen muffins, or halve the receipt for a dozen.

Making variations is as easy as reaching up to the butt'ry shelf. *Raisin muffins:* add 1 cup chopped raisins and 1 tsp. cinnamon to plain muffin receipt. *Date muffins:* add 1 cup chopped dates. Before putting into the oven, sprinkle with 2 Tbs. sugar and ½ tsp. cinnamon mixed together. *Blueberry muffins:* increase sugar in plain muffin receipt to ⅔ cup and add

1 cup blueberries. After baking, while still hot, dip tops in melted butter, then in a mixture of ½ cup sugar and 1 Tbs. cinnamon. For *jam or marmalade muffins:* fill gem pans ⅓ full of plain muffin dough, drop in a teaspoonful of jam or marmalade, then add more dough to ⅔ or ¾ full. Dust with sugar-cinnamon mixture as in date muffins.

To make *shortcake,* use 6 cups mix, ¾ cup sugar, 2 beaten eggs, and ⅔ cup rich milk or light cream. Knead as in biscuits, pat into rounds to fit buttered 8-inch cake pans. Brush tops with melted butter. Bake in hot oven (425°) for 10 to 12 minutes, until browned. Put one circle on serving plate, spread with butter, add sweetened fruit, and place the other circle on top. Cover with whipped cream and add more fruit. Garnish with berries.

JIFFY COFFEE CAKE

Butter an 8-inch round cake tin. Heat oven well (400°).

In a small bowl, blend together with fork 2 Tbs. butter, 2 Tbs. flour, 2 Tbs. brown sugar, ½ tsp. cinnamon, and grated rind of 1 orange. Reserve.

In a larger bowl, mix together 2 cups gem mix, ½ cup sugar, 1 egg, ¾ cup milk, and ¼ cup heavy sour cream. Add ½ cup orange juice. Spread this mixture in the buttered pan. Scatter the cinnamon topping over the top. Bake about 25 minutes. Serve warm in the pan, cut in generous wedges. Let plenty of butter melt into the fragrant pieces.

FLUFFY MUFFINS

Occasionally we run out of the mix and then turn to our favorite receipt for a single batch of gems. It too is subject to interesting variations.

Cream together ¼ cup soft butter, ⅓ cup sugar, 1 beaten egg. Sift 2 cups flour, 4 tsp. baking powder, ½ tsp. salt together. Add to creamed mixture. Add ¾ cup milk and ¼ cup sour cream or heavy sweet cream. Spoon into buttered gem pans. Bake in hot oven (400°) until brown.

Fourth of July

ON the top of the garden shed (it once was a henhouse) is a copper rooster weathervane swinging atop direction letters pointing North, East, South, West. On the Fourth of July from North to South to East to West in all our country Americans are proudly and suitably celebrating this great day. Our rooster is indeed cock of the garden walk as he watches from his perch the industry and festivity going on in our house and garden.

Eating customs across the land may vary considerably, but in New England there is only one way to observe the Fourth properly—with salmon, new peas, and new potatoes. Some say the custom came from the Irish, some say it happens to be just the right season, some say it has always been like this. Whatever the origin, we wouldn't dream of not following the custom.

It's also the season for the first low-bush blueberries on a high sunny slope to begin ripening. There are enough (a cupful is all it takes) for blueberry pancakes for breakfast; if the season is warm and early, sometimes there are also enough for blueberry pie for dinner.

In the morning, a fire is built in the summer-kitchen cookstove, the front lids are removed, and the iron griddle set in. Hand-woven place mats of red are at places around the harvest table, ironstone plates and cups of white, a red-white-and-blue arrangement of geraniums, delphinium, and petunias in the center of the table. To honor the day, the ironstone soup tureen is filled with chilled all-American cranberry juice, the last of last year's cranberries. This is ladled into cups and passed at the table.

Then from the stove come the blueberry pancakes, uniformly four-inch size, light and rich and filled with the plump blue berries that turn red with the baking. The stacks are tall, and they keep coming almost as fast as we can eat. There is plenty of thin-sliced bacon fried crisp, plenty of butter, plenty of maple syrup and of coffee made on the stove in the old white granite pot. The blueberries may run out before the appetites, so make the tender pancakes without them.

When the batter and the coffee are finished, we clear the table, put the ice-cream freezer in operation, and ready the salmon. Dinner is late afternoon, after the parade in the village. If the weather is fine, we set the picnic table for dinner in the garden with Weathervane Rooster keeping watch. Unfold the red tablecloth with hand-tied fringe. Put ironstone plates in place; the salmon comes served on the big blue Canton platter.

Centerpiece and first course is melon and fresh fruit served from a scooped-out watermelon, cold and spiced with fresh mint. Then tiny new potatoes, melted butter, with finely chopped parsley poured over. In another bowl heap up the first peas from the garden, served hot, sweet as sugar.

We like the salmon best whole-poached in bouillon and wine to come melting-tender to the table and served with egg sauce. Homemade bread and butter, pickles, tall glasses of lemonade or iced tea—your choice. Blueberry pie is for dessert if you can find the blueberries, a great triumph when you do; with homemade vanilla ice cream. Or rhubarb pie, perhaps the last pulling of tender stalks for the season.

We fill the glasses again and linger at the table talking over Fourth celebrations of many years ago, until the sun lowers and mosquitoes gather around the ankles. Tonight we'll go to town to watch the fireworks and the young people will stay for the square dancing; maybe the old folks, too.

If it's rainy, we celebrate the Fourth in the summer kitchen and it's Glorious just the same.

BREAKFAST

Iced Cranberry Punch

Crisp Bacon   *Blueberry Pancakes*   *Maple Syrup and Butter*

Pot of Coffee

DINNER

Melon Bowl

Parsleyed New Potatoes   *New Peas*

Whole Poached Salmon with Egg Sauce

Mustard Pickles   *Maple Graham Bread*

Lemonade   *Iced Tea*

Blueberry Pie or Rhubarb Pie

Vanilla Ice Cream

Cranberry punch has been served in New England for many generations. It is eagerly looked forward to from the day in fall when *The Farmer's Almanac* says we may expect frost and Father gathers together the buckets and the clean flour bags in which to put the ripening berries. Everyone goes to the bog, boots knee-high and heavy jackets tight-buttoned, for the wind direction is north, the sky is clear, and frost is indeed a possibility.

Gather the berries by handfuls into buckets, which in turn are emptied into the cloth bags. Sharp marsh grass cuts the hands; toes and noses are getting chilled, but the harvest is gathered with enthusiasm.

At home, spread the berries in trays on the attic floor away from the sunny windows, to continue their ripening. Then pour into jars and crocks and keep in a cool but not freezing place for many, many weeks, to be used as needed.

Fourth of July Breakfast

CRANBERRY PUNCH

Pour into a large kettle equal amounts of cranberries and water, perhaps a gallon of each, and cook until the berries have all popped open. Cool, mash, and strain.

Cook together 6 cups of sugar and 3 cups of water to make a simple syrup. Add the juice of a dozen lemons and 1 tsp. cloves tied in a cheese-cloth bag. Add the cranberry juice and heat to boiling. Remove cloves. Bottle juice and seal.

When ready to serve, pour a quart over ice in a punch bowl or soup tureen, add iced sparkling water to taste.

BLUEBERRY PANCAKES

In a small bowl, whisk together well 1 egg, 1 cup milk, and 2 rounded Tbs. sour cream.

Into a larger bowl, sift together 1 cup flour, ¼ tsp. salt, ½ tsp. mace, 1 Tbs. sugar, and 1 Tbs. baking powder. Into this mixture pour the liquid and beat well with wire whisk or eggbeater. Add 2 Tbs. melted and cooled butter and stir until mixed. If you like pancakes thin, add a bit more milk, perhaps ¼ cup.

Fold in 1 cup blueberries. Drop batter by large spoonfuls onto hot, lightly greased griddle. Brown on one side, turn and brown on the other; turn only once.

The batter is light and delicious even without the blueberries. Serve with plenty of fresh butter and maple syrup in generous pitcherfuls. This receipt makes about a dozen pancakes.

Fourth of July Dinner

MELON BOWL

With a sharp knife, cut out in points the top of a watermelon. Then scoop out the seeds and fruit, leaving a pretty green bowl to fill with melon balls, seeded grapes, pineapple chunks, strawberries, apricot halves, sliced bananas, and seeded Bing cherries. Decorate with sprigs of fresh mint. Chill well before serving.

PARSLEYED NEW POTATOES

Scrub a goodly amount of tiny new potatoes. Cook them in their jackets in boiling salted water to cover just until tender, about 20 minutes. Drain well.

In a small saucepan melt 6 Tbs. butter; mix in ⅓ cup finely minced parsley and juice of ½ lemon. Pour over the hot, unpeeled potatoes in their pan, then arrange around the salmon on a large platter.

NEW PEAS

Who ever has had enough fresh new peas? Shell as many as can be picked fresh and hope that everyone will have a-plenty. Cook them in slightly salted boiling water—as little water as possible, perhaps two cups in a large kettle for 8 cups of peas. If you have to buy them in the market, add ½ tsp. sugar for each cup of peas. Cook just until tender; drain. Add a cupful of thick cream for 8 cups of peas, salt and pepper to taste. Turn into a large nappy, cover, and keep hot at the table.

POACHED SALMON WITH EGG SAUCE

In a fish kettle or other pot large enough to hold the whole or piece of salmon, put enough bouillon ingredients to cover the fish. For 5 or 6 pounds of salmon, this mixture is about right:

2½ qts. water	10 peppercorns
1 small minced onion	1 Tbs. salt

In a small cheesecloth bag, make a bouquet garni of:

½ tsp. whole cloves	2 bay leaves
6 sprigs of parsley	2 sprigs fresh thyme
3 or 4 celery leaves or 1 leaf of lovage	

Add bouquet garni and simmer the bouillon for 20 minutes. Meanwhile, wipe the salmon clean with a cloth and tie it firmly in cheesecloth, with a knot at the top to use in pulling the cooked fish out of the bouillon when it is done. This net keeps the fish firmly in shape while cooking.

Add 2 cups of dry white wine to the simmering bouillon. Lower the fish into the kettle and cover. Bring again to a simmer and cook at simmer for 10 minutes per pound of salmon.

Remove salmon from the pot, lifting onto a large hot platter. Using great care, slip off the cheesecloth. Garnish with the parsleyed new potatoes, sprigs of greenery—parsley, or thyme, mint or watercress—halves of hard-cooked eggs, and thin slices of lemon.

EGG SAUCE

Hard-cook 8 large eggs. Shell and quarter them and reserve four for garnishing the salmon platter. Use the rest for the Egg Sauce.

In a saucepan, melt 1 Tbs. butter, stir in 1 Tbs. flour and cook until bubbly, then add 2 cups bouillon from cooking the fish. Stir and cook until thickened and smooth. Add 3 Tbs. heavy cream and the juice of half a lemon. Fold in the four hard-cooked eggs, chopped. Stir in 1 Tbs. butter. Spoon into sauce tureen and sprinkle with ½ tsp. finely minced parsley. Serve very hot.

AUNT MABEL'S MUSTARD PICKLES

In a large kettle, make a brine of 4 qts. water, 2 cups sack salt (coarse cooking salt). Into this brine put the following vegetables and let stand for 24 hours.

> 1 qt. small (gherkin-sized) cucumbers
> 1 qt. medium cucumbers, sliced ¼-inch thick
> 1 qt. small pickling onions (which can be bought in jars to save peeling the little beasts)
> 1 qt. green tomatoes, cut in quarters or eighths
> 1 head cauliflower divided into small flowerets
> 4 green peppers, cut fine
> 4 sweet red peppers, cut fine

After soaking vegetables for 24 hours, bring to a simmer, then drain.

In a large saucepan, mix 1 cup flour, 6 Tbs. Colman's dry mustard, 1 Tbs. turmeric powder. Make a paste with a little vinegar, then add 1 cup sugar and stir to mix well.

Add enough vinegar to make 2 quarts and cook, stirring constantly, until well mixed and thickened.

In the large kettle in which the vegetables were soaked, bring to a boil 2 cups vinegar and 2 cups water. Add vegetables and cook until tender but not soft; they should be crisp. Drain.

Pour the mustard mixture over the vegetables, and stir with a wooden spoon until well mixed and vegetables are well coated. While still hot, pack in sterilized hot jars and seal. Worth all the trouble.

MAPLE GRAHAM BREAD

So quick and easy to make, so delicious hot, cold, toasted, and for sandwiches, maple graham bread is one of our favorite homemade breads.

Mix together in a bowl:

3 cups graham flour	2 tsp. baking powder
½ cup wheat germ	½ tsp. soda
½ cup white flour	1 tsp. salt

In a large bowl combine:

1½ cup buttermilk or sour milk	½ cup packed brown sugar
½ cup sour cream	½ cup maple syrup

Stir flour mixture into milk mixture with a wooden spoon and mix well. Fold in a cup of raisins if you like. Bake in buttered loaf pan in medium oven (350°) for about 60 minutes, or until it thumps done.

PLAIN ICED TEA

Preheat a pottery teapot by filling with hot water, then pour out the water and put in the tea. Allow 1½ tsp. (or 1½ tea bags) per serving.

Pour boiling fresh water over the tea in the pot, cover, and let stand for at least 10 minutes, or longer to cool somewhat. Strain and pour over ice into a large pitcher, or into glasses filled with ice. Garnish with a thin slice of lemon and a sprig of fresh mint.

BLUEBERRY PIE

Pride in blueberry pie is one of our sins. Make a light pastry for a two-crust pie: Sift together into a bowl 2 cups of flour and ½ tsp. salt. With a pastry blender, cut in ⅓ cup cold butter until well mixed; then cut in another ⅓ cup cold butter or good lard until the mixture is the consistency of small peas. Chill. Over this sprinkle about 6 to 8 Tbs. ice water, a tablespoon at a time, and blend gently with a fork until it is well mixed and can be gathered into two balls with the hands. Gently roll one ball into a circle about an inch larger than the pie plate and ⅛ inch thick. Use just enough flour on the pastry board to keep the dough from sticking; too much flour will make the pastry tough. So will pounding the dough when rolling it out; be gentle. Fit the circle easily into the pie plate without stretching. Trim the edges; the dough should hang over the edge of the plate about an inch.

Roll out the second piece of dough into a rectangle ⅛ inch thick, about 9 inches wide and an inch or two longer than it is wide. Cut with a pie-crimping wheel or sharp knife strips of dough one-half inch wide. About eighteen strips will be needed for a 9-inch pie.

Into the lower pie crust, sprinkle about 2 Tbs. flour and ⅓ cup sugar. Over this put three or more cups of blueberries, including a very few greenish ones for tartness and flavor (or use the juice of half a lemon). Dot generously with butter, 2 more Tbs. flour, and ⅓ cup sugar. Sprinkle with cinnamon.

The top crust is put on by actually weaving the narrow strips in and out. Place nine strips one-half inch apart in one direction. Then in a diagonal direction cross and weave nine strips to make a lattice. Trim the ends. Fold the lower crust over the ends of the strips and flute with your fingertips, building the fluted edge up well from the pie plate so the juice will not boil over.

Dust the top of the pie lightly with granulated sugar. Bake for 15 minutes in a hot oven (450°), then lower the fire and bake until nicely browned and bubbling, perhaps half an hour.

RHUBARB PIE

Prepare crust for pie as in blueberry pie receipt, including the strips.

For the rhubarb filling, wash about a dozen stems of red rhubarb that have had the leaves and end knobs removed. With a sharp knife, cut the rhubarb into half-inch pieces and put into the pastry-lined pie plate.

In a bowl beat two eggs lightly. Add ⅔ cup sugar, 2 Tbs. flour, juice of half a lemon, a pinch of salt, and ¼ tsp. almond flavoring. Stir well together and pour over the rhubarb.

Weave pastry strips in a diamond pattern across the top of the pie as in directions for blueberry pie. Sprinkle lightly with granulated sugar. Bake in a hot oven (450°) for 15 minutes, then reduce heat to moderate (350°) and bake until crust is browned and a knife-point stuck into the rhubarb indicates that it is cooked through and tender. The whites of the eggs in the mixture will puff up between the lattice spaces for a nice effect.

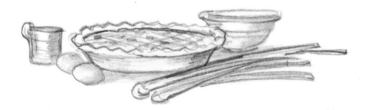

Mountain Cookout

AT the end of the summer come lazy days. Most of the vegetable-garden harvest is in, awaiting only the squash and pumpkin and melon bounty. Grapes are nearly ripe; the last-planted rows of corn are just right for eating, and tomatoes are heavy on the fading vines. Early apples are ready for pies and the Macs will soon be picked. Wild cranberries will have to be gathered soon in the lower bog before the first frost; they will be picked over and packed loosely in big jars to keep in the cellar until they are all gone, well after Christmas. Soon the flaming autumn reds and brilliant golds of the deciduous trees, mingled with the dark greens of the conifers, will weave a tapestry across the hills.

At this time of year there comes an evening when Father will look to the mountain from which he forecasts the weather and then say "Tomorrow will be a good day; shall we go to the mountain?" Everything else is forsaken and preparations for tomorrow begin at once.

Mother puts the beans to soak. Early in the morning they go into the oven to start their cooking. Taken out at the very minute we are ready to leave for the mountain, the pot is wrapped snugly and the beans keep right on cooking.

What a heavenly day to be on the mountain! Sparkling-clear. What fun it is to climb to the top through the shade of the forest where we find ferns and mosses and the patches of shiny green and Christmas red bunchberry. Stumble over the big rocks, skip around the slippery places where a mountain spring bubbles, jump over trees fallen in the great hurricane of 1938. Suddenly we are out in the brilliant sunshine with only the blue of the sky above and around us. We have left the forest behind and are standing on a rock ledge at the very top. Our view of the world below takes our breath away.

In a far-off valley we find our house and barn, and how tiny it looks! Church spires pinpoint all the villages we know for many miles around. Point out Sawyer's apple barn, Ruth's muster field, Sanborn's hilltop house. We can see familiar ponds and lakes, and the river winds its lazy late-summer way among the farms and woods and hills. We can see the high peaks of Vermont's Green Mountains and our own White Mountains. If only we were a bit taller, perhaps we could see the Atlantic!

Someone has stayed below at the picnic site to watch the hardwood fire burn to coals and, at just the proper time, hands are cupped to make a horn for the call to dinner, which brings everyone down from the top much faster than the going up. We can smell the steak and the coffee and are ready for hearty eating.

The picnic table is laden, much of it from our own land. Hot soup is poured from the thermos into blue granite cups. Father carves the thick sirloin; baked beans rich with salt pork are ladled onto the blue graniteware plates. Tomatoes and cucumbers are sliced into a bowl and then dusted with fresh tarragon—help yourself. Tear off a piece of warm French bread with garlic butter. Fresh corn roasted in the husk is its own course—how many ears can you eat? Finally the pie basket is opened and green-apple pie is cut in wide pieces, with a slice of cheese from our own Crossroads Country Store atop. Pour steaming coffee from the pot on the fire or have a cup of fresh milk.

After the dinner is over and the fires are carefully drenched, we sit on the rocks and visit. We talk of how Mountain Day was when Grandmother was a girl, when the trip was made by farm wagon and horses and took many more hours. We watch the evening haze spread as the sun sets over the land below. The lowering light is mirrored in lakes across the miles; the hills grow pink and purple and black as the deep of the sky pushes down to the horizon.

MOUNTAIN COOKOUT

Thermos of Hot Tomato Soup
Baked Beans   Sirloin Steak
Fresh Sliced Tomatoes and Cucumbers with Tarragon
French Bread with Garlic Butter   Corn Roasted in the Husk
Apple Pie with Cheese
Picnic Pot of Coffee   Cold Fresh Milk

HOT TOMATO SOUP

Wash and cut in quarters 1 peck tomatoes. Peel and quarter 4 onions. Cut ½ bunch of celery into pieces. Seed and dice a whole green pepper.

Put these ingredients into a large kettle. Add 1 quart water, 1½ cups sugar, 5 or 6 whole cloves, 4 bay leaves, ¼ cup cider vinegar, and 2 Tbs. Worcestershire sauce.

Bring to a boil and simmer all ingredients together for an hour. Add salt and freshly ground pepper to taste. Remove from heat and put through a food mill or sieve.

Reheat to boiling, pour into sterilized quart jars and seal. May be served ice-cold as a cocktail, or piping hot as a soup. For a picnic, heat well, pour into a large Thermos jug, and pour into mugs.

BAKED BEANS

Wash 2 pounds (4 cups) dried pea beans and soak for 6 or 8 hours or overnight in water to cover. Add to the beans 1 tsp. soda and bring to a boil. Simmer until tender or until the skins open when blown on. Drain the beans and put into the Dorchester pottery (2-quart size) beanpot. Poke in halves of 2 bay leaves. Push into the pot ½ lb. lean salt pork cut in generous pieces; save one piece for the top of the pot.

Mix together and pour into the pot:

½ cup maple syrup (or ½ cup brown sugar or molasses)	1 tsp. Colman's dry mustard
½ tsp. ginger powder	1 small minced onion
	2 tsp. salt

Stir beans gently to mix ingredients. Pour boiling water into the pot to cover the beans. Cover the pot.

Bake in a slow even (about 200°) for at the least 6 hours, longer if possible. Add a little more water if they cook dry.

SIRLOIN STEAK

To serve eight hungry people, have two aged sirloin steaks cut 1¾ to 2 inches thick. Slash the edges to prevent curling.

Build a good fire of hardwood sticks about as big as your wrist, and let them burn vigorously until they are red-hot coals. Hickory, oak, and maple work best; birch burns fast and hot and is a good fire-starter.

When the coals are just right, grease a wire broiler generously with a piece of beef suet and place the steaks on the broiler close enough to the coals to sear. When well-browned, turn and sear the other side. This should take about five minutes a side. If the steaks have been trimmed of excess fat, they will not drip exceedingly.

Raise the broiler 3 or 4 inches and turn the steaks, cooking for another ten minutes each side—more or less according to your taste. Remove from fire, sprinkle with salt and freshly ground black pepper. Place steaks on a clean board for carving.

FRESH TOMATOES AND CUCUMBERS WITH TARRAGON

Combine in a wooden bowl quartered fresh unpeeled tomatoes and cucumber fingers which have been cut lengthwise. If the cucumber is a large one, cut the long slices in half. Dust the contents of the bowl with salt, freshly ground pepper, and minced tarragon leaves. May be eaten with the fingers.

FRENCH BREAD WITH GARLIC BUTTER

Into a generous bowl put 1 package dry yeast in 1 cup warm water and stir until yeast dissolves. Stir in 3 Tbs. soft butter, 1 tsp. salt, and ¼ cup cold water. With a wooden spoon stir into the yeast mixture 4 cups flour, 2 cups at a time. Mix well, using hands if necessary. Work into a ball, place on a lightly floured board, and cover with towel for ten minutes. Knead with vigor until smooth and no longer sticky. Smooth into a round and put into a greased bowl; cover with dampened clean dishtowel. Let rise in warm place until double, about 2 hours. Punch down, cover again, and let rise 20 to 30 minutes. Shape into a rectangle about 15 inches long on a lightly floured board. Roll it up tightly, seal the edges and turn under the ends, tapering the loaf. Place on lightly greased cooky sheet. Cut several slashes across top of the loaf with a sharp knife. Let rise an hour uncovered.

Brush with water, put in medium-hot oven (375°). Bake 20 minutes, then brush with an egg white whisked together with 2 Tbs. water, and return to the oven to bake until brown, about 20 to 25 minutes.

At the picnic, cut loaf in slices almost through. Spread the slices apart a little and spread with garlic butter made by crushing half a clove of garlic into ¼ lb. soft butter and mixing well. Wrap the loaf in foil and place on the grill or close to the coals, but do not burn. Heat about 15 minutes, turning several times.

CORN ROASTED IN THE HUSK

Pick the corn at the last possible minute before leaving home. On arrival at the mountain, lay the corn in the hollowed log which catches the spring water (or stand in a bucket of fresh cold water). When ready to cook the corn, remove silks from all the ears. Peel back but do not remove husks and spread corn with soft or melted butter. Replace husks.

When the steak has been removed from the coals, place the ears either on a grill close to the coals or right on the coals. Turn often; roast for about 20 minutes. Heap on the table and serve with plenty of salt, pepper, and butter.

APPLE PIE

Make pastry (p. 97) and line a 9-inch pie plate, leaving a width of pastry 1 inch larger than the plate. Peel, core, and slice tart apples to make about 6 cups. Arrange slices in the pie plate, firming well. If apples are not tart, squeeze a half lemon over the slices.

Mix together ¼ cup brown sugar, ½ cup white sugar, 1 Tbs. flour, and ½ tsp. cinnamon. Sprinkle this over the apples and grate some nutmeg over the top. Dot generously with butter.

Roll out the top crust, slash the center with a sharp knife in a little design. Put crust over the apple mixture. With fingers, apply a little cold water around the edge of the crust, fold the lower edge up over the edge of the top crust and flute with fingers to make a nice edging. Brush top crust with cream and sprinkle white granulated sugar over it.

Bake in a hot oven (425°) for 15 minutes, then lower the heat (350°) and continue baking until brown and apples are tender. May be tested by sticking a paring knife through one of the slashes in the top crust to see if apples are done.

Serve with cheese or with thick country cream.

PICNIC COFFEE

Into a thin clean muslin bag measure 1 Tbs. coffee for each measuring cup of water to be used, plus an extra Tbs. for the pot. Tie loosely, leaving room for the water to penetrate and the coffee grounds to expand, and take the coffee to the picnic in this bag. Plan to get two servings or coffee-cupfuls from each measuring cup of water. Use a generous granite coffee pot. Ours is a gallon size; we use 12 cups of water and a generous three-fourths measuring cup of coffee (13 Tbs.).

When ready to make the coffee, measure or pour the cups of clear cold water into the pot and put it on the fire. When this comes to a boil, put the coffee, bag and all, into the pot and shake in a wisp of salt. Bring to a boil again, then put on the back of the fire to simmer gently until ready to serve.

Birthdays

ONCE upon a time, long long ago (it seems) there was a little girl with long black curls and a freckled pug nose who wore an enormous hair ribbon, for whom her birthday was the most exciting day of the year except Christmas. From the moment she awakened in the morning until she went to sleep at night, she was filled with excitement and happiness. Because she was the youngest in the family, everyone helped make this her special day. There were presents at breakfast, something she wanted very much like new hair ribbons, clothes for her doll, and always a silver dollar for every year of her life with an extra to grow on. Once there was a little camera just the right size, and another birthday there was a real gold watch with her initials on the back.

And of course because Birthday People always chose what they wanted most to eat for dinner, there was something very special about that, too. The little girl always chose the dessert she loved even more than cake. It was just called Pink Pudding. It always looked very beautiful turned out on the pink Haviland chop plate, with pink candles lighted around it and a garnish of strawberries or little pink rosebuds or sweet peas. Best of all, she was allowed to have all she could eat of it, which was quite a lot. (It still is, many years later.)

Mother's birthday favorite was her own Lady Margaret Jane Cake, a white cake with pink frosting, and raspberry cream between the layers. It was always baked with a rose geranium leaf in the bottom of the pans, and the delicate perfume flavored every bite.

Brother invariably chose Fudge Cake, and he liked plenty of chocolate frosting with butternuts in it. There was no waiting for dinner to have this, for he always came home from play with an unpredictable number of his school friends to share it. Once he invited his whole schoolroom to come, with no warning to Mother, who fortunately had plenty of bread for peanut butter-and-jelly sandwiches, and plenty of apples and cookies in the butt'ry.

Father was cagey about his age and his favorite birthday treat was nothing that would hold candles. It was rare roast beef with Yorkshire pudding, and lemon meringue pie. He was the only one in the family with enough influence to have *two* favorite dishes served on his birthday.

Our family favorite birthday dishes haven't changed in many years, and they are all still very special.

Pink Pudding

Lady Margaret Jane Cake

Fudge Cake

Newport Roast Beef with
   Yorkshire Pudding

Lemon Meringue Pie

PINK PUDDING

In a tin (or aluminum) cup soak 1 Tbs. unflavored gelatin in ¼ cup cold water until soft, then melt it over boiling water until gelatin is very thin and liquid.

Squeeze the juice of 2 oranges and 1 lemon and pour it over 1 cup sugar with the grated rind of 1 orange added. Stir until sugar is well dissolved. Add ½ tsp. vanilla, ¼ tsp. almond flavoring, and a few grains of salt. Add some pink food coloring and mix well.

Whip 1 cup heavy cream very stiff, then fold in the fruit-juice mixture, and last the melted gelatin. Pour into a small fancy mold or into individual molds and put in the ice-box for several hours or until well set.

This receipt makes a serving for four, and may well be doubled to put into a larger fancy mold. When serving, invert on a pretty plate. Tiny birthday candles may be placed around the top of the pudding. Fresh flowers arranged around the edge of the plate add to the festivity.

LADY MARGARET JANE CAKE

Butter generously and flour three 8-inch round cake pans. In the bottom of each lay several perfect rose geranium leaves.

Sift and then measure 3 cups cake flour. Add ¾ tsp. salt and 3 tsp. baking powder and sift again 3 times.

Cream ¾ cup soft butter until very light, then add gradually 2 cups sugar and continue beating until well mixed and fluffy.

Add sifted dry ingredients to the creamed mixture alternately with ½ cup rich milk and ½ cup water, beating lightly until smooth. Add 1½ tsp. vanilla and ½ tsp. almond flavoring if no rose geranium leaves are available.

Beat until very stiff 6 egg whites and fold lightly into the cake mixture, making sure the batter is mixed together well.

Pour batter into the three prepared pans and bake in moderate oven (350°) about 30 minutes, or until cake is firm to a light touch of the fingers in the center of each cake. Cool on cake racks; remove rose geranium leaves.

RASPBERRY CREAM FILLING

Whip ½ cup heavy cream until very stiff. Beat into the cream ½ cup firm raspberry jam. Spread on tops of two of the layers of white cake. Set the third layer on, then frost the whole cake with Fluffy Frosting.

FLUFFY FROSTING

Into a saucepan put 1 cup sugar and ½ cup water. Cook together for several minutes, covering the pan. Uncover and when syrup spins a thin thread 6 or 8 inches long, remove from the fire and let cool only until mixture stops bubbling.

Beat 2 egg whites until foamy, add ¼ tsp. cream of tartar, and continue to beat until stiff enough to hold a peak.

In a thin steady stream, add the syrup to the egg whites. Do not scrape sides of the pan, but use all the syrup that will pour without scraping. Continue beating vigorously until the frosting will hold stiff peaks.

At this point add ¾ tsp. vanilla, ½ tsp. almond flavoring, and enough red food coloring to make a pretty pink color. Mix and stir together.

Frost sides of cake, then pile the balance onto the top, swirling with the spoon. Let the cake stand to cool and to set the frosting.

FUDGE CAKE FOR BROTHER

Melt 3 squares unsweetened chocolate in a small saucepan, add ½ cup water, and cook and stir together until well blended. Remove from heat and cool slightly.

In a large bowl, cream ½ cup soft butter until fluffy, gradually beat in 1⅔ cups sugar, and beat well until creamy and smooth. Add chocolate. Add 2 jumbo (or 3 medium) eggs and beat in thoroughly.

Sift 2 cups flour and measure into a bowl 2 cups plus 2 Tbs. of this flour. Add ½ tsp. soda, 2½ tsp. baking powder, and ½ tsp. salt.

Sift the flour mixture into the creamed mixture by thirds, alternating with ⅔ cup milk to which 2 generous Tbs. sour cream have been added. Add 2 tsp. vanilla. Fold these ingredients very lightly into the creamed mixture and continue folding lightly until all the flour has been moistened. Do not beat.

Pour the batter into two 8- or 9-inch cake pans that have been generously buttered and floured. Bake in a moderate oven (350°) for 35 minutes or until the cake shrinks from the sides of the pan or springs back when lightly touched with a finger. Cool for 10 minutes in the pan; invert onto cake racks to cool thoroughly. Frost with fudge frosting.

FUDGE FROSTING

Melt 3 squares unsweetened chocolate in the top of a double boiler. Beat in 2 Tbs. hot water and 1½ to 2 cups sifted powdered sugar. Blend until smooth. Add one small egg and beat again. Add 4 Tbs. soft butter a little at a time and beat again until smooth. Remove from heat and add 1 tsp. vanilla.

With a small spatula, spread a thin layer of frosting on top of one layer of cake; put the other layer on top of it. Spread a thin layer of frosting around sides of cake.

Add ½ cup coarsely chopped butternuts or black walnuts to the balance of the frosting and spread generously on top of the cake. Put one red-and-white-striped large birthday candle in the center of the cake. This is to wish on.

NEWPORT ROAST BEEF

Rich brown gravy doesn't come from the newfangled slow oven way of roasting prime ribs of beef. Father would consider it ridiculous. He calls his favorite birthday dish Newport Roast Beef because of its elegance. He thought it small economy and flavor ever to cook anything less than four ribs. We agree.

Prepare (or have prepared by the family butcher) an aged prime four-rib roast of beef. It should be trimmed of excess fat while leaving a reasonable blanket of fat over the top. Remove the short ribs and save them to braise with vegetables for another meal. Wipe with damp cloth and season all over with salt and pepper. Then dust lightly with flour, turning on all sides and rubbing in the flour and seasonings. Place fat side up on rack in open roasting pan and place in a very hot (475°) oven. Beginners should use a meat thermometer inserted through the top center of the roast into the center of the meat, making certain the thermometer does not touch a rib. Roast at high temperature for a half hour, then reduce the fire (350°) for half an hour; reduce still more (300°) to complete the roasting. Allow about 18 minutes per pound (ending up with 140° on the meat thermometer) for rare roast beef. The roast will be crispy brown outside and rare in the center.

Plan that the roast should be done about a half-hour before serving time. When removed from the oven, place roast on a hot platter and cover lightly to keep hot.

YORKSHIRE PUDDING

For eight servings, beat well with rotary beater 2 large eggs, add 1 cup milk and 3 Tbs. beef drippings from the roasting pan, then beat again thoroughly. Add ½ tsp. salt and then beat in gradually and thoroughly ¾ cup flour.

Put 1 Tbs. beef drippings into each cup of a gem pan (or into eight glass custard cups which for ease of handling have been set into a gem pan). Put into hot oven (450°) to heat for 5 minutes, then pour in the batter. Bake at high heat (450°) for 10 minutes, reduce fire to 350° and bake another 20 minutes, until puffed high and well browned. Remove from gem cups and bring to the table arranged around the roast.

Pudding batter may also be baked in a cake pan in which 4 or 5 Tbs. beef drippings have been placed. In this case, when puffed, brown, and crisp, cut into pieces and serve very hot.

LEMON MERINGUE PIE

Father liked a good fresh lemony taste to his pie, and on his birthday extra egg whites were usually added to the meringue for a mountainous gala effect.

For two pies, prepare the receipt for pie crust (p. 97). Fit the rolled dough into two 8-inch pie plates, flute edges high, prick the pastry shells well with a fork, and bake in a hot oven (425°) until nicely browned. Cool.

In a saucepan, mix 1½ cups sugar and ⅓ cup cornstarch (or ½ cup flour). Add a pinch (¼ tsp.) of salt. Add 1¼ cups boiling water gradually and stir until smooth. Bring to a boil, stir constantly, and cook until very thick. Remove from fire for a moment. Beat lightly the yolks of 4 eggs and stir in a little of the hot mixture. Then stir this slowly into the balance of the hot mixture. Add grated rind and juice of 1½ lemons and cook again until well heated and very thick, stirring vigorously. Remove from stove and add a good lump of butter (about 2 Tbs.). Beat until smooth and butter is melted. Pour custard into the baked cooled crust.

MERINGUE

For two 8-inch pies, use whites of 6 large eggs. Beat the whites until frothy with 1 tsp. lemon juice. Add ¾ cup sugar a little at a time, and beat to very stiff peaks. Pile onto the warm filling, spooning meringue right to the edge of the crust. Bake in a hot oven (400°) until nicely browned. Cool gradually and thoroughly for several hours before serving.

Thimble Tea and the Quilting Bee

IN Grandmother's day Thimble Tea was a gathering of her friends once a month or so, held in turn in their own homes. It was always a sewing meeting; occasionally there was a day when the quilting frames Grandfather had made were set up and a quilt was stretched and tacked on. Some of the ladies were better quilters than others, but all worked equally diligently if a quilt was to be made to sell for the church. There were friendship quilts, on which each lady wrote her name in the center of a pretty block and embroidered it in colored thread. There were patchwork quilts, crazy quilts made with scraps of many colors, and appliqué quilts, all with pleasant names like Log Cabin, Rose of Sharon, Turkey Tracks, Martha Washington's Flower Garden.

No one remembers who gave Thimble Tea its name, but it was never just tea. It was an all-day meeting, and the hostess served a lunch and later in the afternoon a cup of tea with cookies. After that the sewing was put away and at suppertime the husbands appeared to share in the "covered dishes" (now we call them casseroles) and desserts the ladies had brought with them. Kitty whist was the evening's entertainment—not a very serious game, for there was too much visiting to do.

Grandmother's luncheon specialty was chicken salad, for chickens were always at hand. We still make it for our version of Thimble Tea when "the girls" gather for an all-day session of sewing.

And we still use Grandfather's quilting frames, much battered and patched from so many years of use. Our beds are quilt-covered; the blanket chest is filled with lovingly folded reminders of several generations of quiltmakers and our linen chest with hand-embroidered linens made on Thimble Tea day. All are used with pride and care.

LUNCHEON AND TEA

Thimble Tea Chicken Salad

Marmalade Muffins   Peach Pickles

Apple Crisp

Pot of Coffee

Four o'clock Tea with

"Grandma" Ballantyne's Scotch Shortbread

THIMBLE TEA CHICKEN SALAD

Cook a large chicken according to the directions for Chicken Consommé (p. 39). Reserve the broth for other use. Cut the meat into generous cubes to provide about 4 or 5 cups of chicken pieces.

Put the cubed chicken pieces into a large bowl. Add ½ cup finely chopped celery. Then add a generous cupful of any *one* of the following:

tiny seedless white grapes; halved seeded Muscat grapes; small cubes of fresh or canned drained pineapple; whole drained cooked sweetened cranberries. Turn over together carefully with a large fork and spoon to distribute evenly.

In another bowl, mix together thoroughly ½ tsp. Colman's dry mustard, 2 tsp. salt and a generous sprinkle of freshly ground pepper, ½ cup rich cream, and 1 cup mayonnaise.

Fold the two mixtures together lightly. Put in the ice-box to chill thoroughly for several hours. Serve in lettuce cups on a luncheon plate; garnish with salted almonds, mint or watercress, and a peach pickle. Pass the Marmalade Muffins, and butter curls in a cut-glass dish.

MARMALADE MUFFINS

Make 2 dozen Marmalade Muffins from mix according to the directions given on pages 87–88. Before putting in the oven, mix 6 Tbs. sugar with the grated rind of 2 oranges and dust over the tops.

Or make them this way:

Into a large bowl put ½ cup soft butter and cream until fluffy. Add ½ cup sugar and beat until light. Add 2 eggs and beat again.

Sift together 3½ cups sifted flour, 1 tsp. salt, 3 Tbs. baking powder. Combine 1½ cups milk and ½ cup heavy sour cream. Add flour mixture to butter mixture alternately with the milk, stirring lightly just until mixed together.

Spoon mixture into greased gem pans until half-full. With a teaspoon, put marmalade into each; then spoon more batter on top, filling to about two-thirds. Spoon over the top of each muffin a little of the sugar-orange-rind mixture. Bake in a hot oven (400°) until browned, about 25 minutes.

PEACH PICKLES

Choose about 4 quarts of small perfect ripe peaches. Put them into a strainer and scald in a kettle of boiling water for 30 seconds; rinse in cold water and slip the skins off the fruit.

In a kettle, boil together for 15 minutes 3 cups light cider vinegar and 6 cups sugar, 4 pieces of whole cinnamon, and 1 Tbs. whole cloves. Put enough peaches to fill one jar into the syrup and cook until tender.

Pack into wide-mouth jars that have been washed and rinsed in hot water. Into each jar put a few cloves. Pour hot syrup into the jar to over-flowing, wipe edge of jar quickly with clean damp cloth and seal immediately. This makes about 8 pint jars of pickles.

APPLE CRISP

Butter a baking dish well. Slice into it 8 tart juicy apples. Grate rind of one lemon over the top of the apples and sprinkle with the juice of the lemon.

In a bowl, mix together:

1 cup brown sugar	½ tsp. ground ginger
1 cup flour	1 tsp. cinnamon
½ cup soft butter	½ tsp. salt

Sprinkle seasoned mixture over apples. Bake in medium oven (350°) for 35 minutes, or until apples are soft. Serve with heavy cream or ice cream. Equally good hot or cold.

"GRANDMA" BALLANTYNE'S SCOTCH SHORTBREAD

"Grandma" Ballantyne was one of the intrepid Scots who pioneered in the West. She smoked a clay pipe, warmed herself in the rugged Plains winters with a very occasional nip from a brown bottle, and wore a long, black, full dress. She was Grandma to everyone who knew her, and her shortbread was as famous as her thick Scots burr and dry humor. Her receipt came to us through Western cousins. Like many of our *Buttery Book* receipts, this one listed only the ingredients. Good cooks were expected to have the good sense to know how to put them together. For first-timers, however, we give instructions, as we have done in other *Buttery Book* receipts.

1 lb. butter	½ lb. superfine sugar (1 cup)
1 lb. flour (4 cups)	

Sift flour and sugar together. Work the butter into the flour and sugar with fingertips, then knead until thoroughly blended and smooth. Break into two pieces. Pat each piece separately about ½ inch thick onto a lightly sugared board. Cut into little squares (about 2 inches). Pinch up the edges with the fingers to flute, prick well with a fork, and bake on an ungreased cooky sheet in a medium oven (325°) for 25 or 30 minutes. These rich cookies do not expand, and they should not be browned.

At Christmastime, we double or triple the receipt and vary the cookies by rolling into the tops grated orange peel or finely ground almonds or coriander seeds. But this was not "Grandma" Ballantyne's way.

Hallowe'en

HALLOWE'EN is many autumn things, none of them very spooky. Not that we have no ghosts. A ghost lives in our house who wouldn't scare a youngster if he could help it. Once or twice, when he has turned himself into a bat, he has given some of the grown-ups a few bad moments. He only does this when the butt'ry window has been left open at night and it's his way of showing how careless we can be.

Hallowe'en is the last of the flowers in the garden, as the chrysanthemums and calendulas bravely outlast all the tender blossoms. It is gathering in of the pumpkins and squashes and putting the gardens to bed. It is frosty nights with brilliant stars and sometimes a cold north wind to remind us to put on storm windows. It is raking leaves and filling the woodbox. It is building a fire in the cookstove to warm the kitchen in the morning. It is making gingerbread and baking apples and planning the mincemeat.

It is the time to fill the butt'ry cooky and candy jars and to make the

121

sweet cider. It is the time to decorate the barn with cornshocks and with scooped-out pumpkins and funny-shaped squashes with cutout faces of leering goblins and with black cats and witches on broomsticks. It is the time to frost pumpkin tarts with whipped cream and to caramel apples on a stick and to fill the washtub with water for bobbing Macs. It is the time to get into the attic trunks for costumes and to start the record player for square dancing and choose your partner, line up here for the Hallowe'en party.

HALLOWE'EN TREATS

Caramel Apples Taffy
Hattie Hoyt's Walnut Brittle
Gingersnaps Hearty Sandwiches
Pumpkin Tarts with Whipped Cream
Popcorn Balls
Sweet Cider

CARAMEL APPLES

Combine in the top of a large double boiler 4 cups sugar, 2 cups water, and ½ tsp. cream of tartar. Put the pan directly over low heat. Cook and stir until sugar is dissolved and the syrup boils. Cook without stirring to crack stage (300°–310°). "Crack stage" in cooking candy is reached when a little of the hot syrup dropped into a cup of cold water will break when hit against the side of the cup. Remove from heat immediately and stir in 1 tsp. lemon juice or light cider vinegar. Add several drops red or yellow food coloring. Put pan into warm (not hot) water to keep syrup from getting too stiff while dipping apples.

Dip into the syrup small perfect nicely colored apples with sturdy stems; coat well and then dip quickly into ice water, and set to harden on a well-buttered cooky sheet. If the apples do not have good stems, punch lollipop sticks down into the stem ends before dipping into the syrup.

TAFFY FOR PULLING

In a generous saucepan, put ¾ cup brown sugar, 1 cup white sugar, 2 cups light molasses, and 1 cup water. Stir together and keep stirring slowly while cooking over low heat until it reaches the crack stage (300°–310°). Remove from the fire, add 4 Tbs. butter, a small pinch of soda, and a large pinch of salt. Mix together quickly and pour onto a large greased platter. Let cool enough to handle. With buttered fingers, pull the candy until light and firm, then stretch into a rope, twist and cut into pieces with buttered scissors.

HATTIE HOYT'S WALNUT BRITTLE

In a saucepan, combine 2 cups sugar, ½ cup good vinegar, and ½ cup butter. Bring slowly to a boil, then continue boiling until it reaches hard crack stage (300°–310°).

Butter a rectangular cake pan and scatter over it ½ cup chopped walnuts. Pour candy over the walnuts in the cake pan, and let cool and harden. When well hardened, turn pan upside down, rap sharply against the table; the candy will come out in a sheet. Break into pieces.

GINGERSNAPS

Cream 1 cup butter; add 1½ cups brown sugar, ½ cup molasses, and beat all together thoroughly. Sift together 4 cups flour, a pinch of salt, 1 tsp. soda, 1 tsp. cinnamon, and 1 tsp. powdered ginger.

Add dry ingredients to the creamed mixture alternately with ¼ cup strong black coffee. Mix well with wooden spoon, then chill for several hours.

Roll on lightly floured board about ⅛ inch thick. Cut with round floured 2-inch cooky cutter, sprinkle with sugar, place on buttered cooky sheets, and bake about 10 minutes in moderate oven (350°). Or break off dough in pieces the size of a thimble, roll into a little ball, flatten a bit, dust with sugar, and bake. Makes plenty of cookies.

HEARTY SANDWICHES

Cut whole-wheat and white bread into slices of medium thickness. Spread with softened butter and an assortment of fillings: cooked ham, roast beef, or chicken put through the meat grinder, seasoned and mixed with a little mayonnaise; tuna fish and finely chopped celery mixed with mayonnaise; cheese and peanut butter combined with sweet pickle relish. Trim crusts and cut diagonally in two.

PUMPKIN TARTS WITH WHIPPED CREAM

Make a receipt of Pie Crust (p. 97). Divide into about four balls and roll one at a time on lightly floured board. Cut into rounds with a large fluted cooky cutter (about 4-inch diameter) and press into the cups of a gem pan. Prick with fork. Bake in a hot oven (425°) for 15 minutes, then in a moderate oven (350°) until browned.

Into a saucepan put ⅔ cup brown sugar, ½ tsp. cinnamon, ½ tsp. ginger, ½ tsp. nutmeg, and ½ tsp. salt. Add 1 Tbs. unflavored gelatin and mix well.

In a small bowl beat 3 egg yolks; add ¾ cup light cream and mix well. Stir this into the saucepan and cook until the mixture boils, stirring slowly. When it boils, take from fire and fold in 1½ cups cooked pumpkin. Chill until the mixture just begins to jell but is not set.

Whip 3 egg whites till frothy, add 3 Tbs. white sugar, and beat to stiff peaks. Fold the pumpkin mixture carefully and thoroughly into the whites and spoon into the cooled tart shells. Chill thoroughly. Just before serving, whip 1 cup heavy cream until very stiff. Flavor to taste with vanilla sugar (p. 12) and spoon a heaping tablespoonful onto each tart. May be eaten with a fork or at a Hallowe'en party out of hand.

POPCORN BALLS

Into a large bowl pour about five quarts of freshly popped corn and keep in a warm oven while making the syrup.

In a buttered saucepan, combine:

1½ cups hot water	½ cup light corn syrup
2 cups sugar	1 tsp. vinegar
½ tsp. salt	

Bring to a boil and cook to the hard-ball stage (when syrup forms a firm hard ball when dropped in cup of cold water or 270° on a candy thermometer).

Pour the syrup over the warm popped corn and mix well. While warm, form into balls and put on cooky sheets to cool. (Buttering the hands lightly makes this job easier.)

Pile the finished popcorn balls into big wooden salad bowls for passing around.

Thanksgiving

IT is said that the original Plymouth Colony Thanksgiving was a three-day celebration and harvest feast. We have simmered it down to one day of feasting, but there is a great building-up of activity and butt'ry bounty for days beforehand for this special occasion in New England.

Indian Summer days have long gone. Banks of leaves have been drifted into corners by a blustery north wind and there is a touch of winter across the fields as the autumn's first snow blankets the corn stubble. The bird-feeders are busy; a brace of pheasant looks for a handout in the barnyard. The cattle and horses are bedded warmly in the barn, and the fireplace in the Old Kitchen blazes with warmth every evening at dusk. For weeks the family has gathered here for the comfortable and satisfying tasks of the late year. The children are busy with homework; when it is done, they crack butternuts with flatirons or make candles or pull taffy, or read exciting books such as A *Tale of Two Cities* or *Treasure Island*.

In the butt'ry, the mincemeat has been made and put into crocks and some has already been baked into pies for the freezer, a delightful change from the days when a housewife stacked her pies in the unheated butt'ry to stay frozen until she was ready to use them. A keg of cider is in the cellar to take on just a touch of fizz for Thanksgiving. The pigs have been divided into chops, sausage, head cheese, sides of bacon, and hams, and the salt pork is in a crock weighted down with a rock on a plate. The best and fattest turkey in the yard has been killed and is ready for stuffing.

Thanksgiving is a family day, and the aunts and uncles and cousins who are within coming distance begin arriving a day or two ahead. By Wednesday night everyone has found a place to put his toothbrush and a place to sleep. It's early to bed, for tomorrow the men are up long before the peep of dawn to go a-hunting. They are home in time for late breakfast, and the game they have bagged is hung in the barn for admiring and curing. There isn't a very impressive array these days, but when Grandfather led the hunters, they came home laden with deer, partridge, pheasant, squirrels, rabbits, ducks, and geese, enough to share with the neighbors too.

The women have a busy time, words spilling out to catch up on family news as fingers fly to peel potatoes and onions and apples, mash the squash, set the table in all its Thanksgiving finery. Someone presses out the long-folded yellow linen cloth hand-woven in the truly American honeysuckle pattern, with napkins to match. A wooden bowl of fresh fruits forms the centerpiece. The yellow candles we have hand-dipped are tall in pewter candlesticks and will soon be ablaze with golden light.

For hours the turkey has been roasting in its tin oven before the fireplace in the Old Kitchen. A bowl of basting sauce with a brush stands ready, and anyone who goes past gives the slowly browning bird a turn of the spit handle and a baste. No cookstove turkey could possibly compare with this traditional turkey on the spit, and everyone takes credit for doing the best job of basting.

BREAKFAST UNDER THE APPLE TREE

FOURTH OF JULY

MOUNTAIN COOKOUT

BIRTHDAYS

THIMBLE TEA AND THE QUILTING BEE

HALLOWE'EN

THANKSGIVING

CHRISTMAS

In New England it is considered only proper that a hospitable Thanksgiving hostess have three kinds of crimp-edged pie ready in the butt'ry. Thick cream may be spooned on or yellow cheese sliced thin on top.

At last the candles are lighted; the family is called to dinner. We remember a line from *Lorna Doone*—"The pleasure of the mouth is the nose before"—a tantalizing aroma and a splendor to the look of the board. The table is groaning and soon everyone around it will be, too. Find your name on a place card, Father (and the turkey, resplendent on the turkey platter garnished with spiced red apples, parsley, and paper spats) always at the head of the table; then stand behind your chair for a moment.

It was Grandfather with his splendid baritone voice who initiated our custom of singing the "Doxology" before being seated at the Thanksgiving table. We can hear him now as he led the family in the familiar hymn, voices all ringing in grateful praise and thanks: "Praise God from Whom all blessings flow. . . ."

THANKSGIVING DINNER

Oyster Cocktail

Hearth-roasted Turkey with Spiced Red Crab-apples

Sausage and Sage Dressing   Giblet Gravy

Creamed Onions   Mashed Potatoes   Squash Soufflé

Eben's Cranberry Sherbet

Cranberry Sauce   Celery Sticks   Pickled Peaches

Cornbread   Fresh Butter

Pumpkin Pie   Apple Pie (p. 104)

Mince Pie with Brandy Hard Sauce

Thick Cream   Yellow Cheese

Champagne Cider   Coffee   Orange Liqueur

OYSTER COCKTAIL

Choose 4 fresh oysters in the shell for each serving. If the shell is open, discard it. Wash well in cold water. Open the shells by forcing a short knife in. Cut the muscle that attaches the oyster to the upper shell (the flat side). Then cut the muscle on the lower (deep) shell.

Into cocktail glasses shred a little crisp lettuce. Place four oysters on this bed in each glass. Squeeze a few drops of lemon juice over oysters. Grind a few grains of black pepper over them. Top with a generous tablespoonful of sauce.

OYSTER COCKTAIL SAUCE

Into a bowl put 1 cup chili sauce, juice of 1 large lemon, a few drops of Tabasco and 1 Tbs. Worcestershire sauce. Add 1 tsp. celery salt and as much horseradish as you like. Mix together and chill well before serving.

HEARTH-ROASTED TURKEY

There is a *Buttery Book* that gives such excellent directions for roasting meats before the fire that we will let it speak for itself. An ancient book, brown with age and frayed from use, it is *The Housekeeper's Book by a Lady.*

"The kitchen chimney should be frequently swept; the cook should, once or twice a week, sweep it as far as she can reach. Ever so little soot falling will sometimes spoil a dinner. See that the spit be brightly clean and take care to run it through the meat in the right place at once; for the more the meat is perforated, the greater chance there will be for the escape of the juices. There is a great nicety required in spitting, in order that the roast may be accurately balanced.

"Twice, or if the roast be a large one, oftener, stir the fire, bring forward the hot coals and put fresh fuel at the back. Be careful that cinders do not reach the dripping-pan. With a clear, strong fire (and meat cannot be well roasted without a strong fire), time allowed for gradual cooking, and by careful bastings, a cook may insure for her roastings that fine brown color, to produce which is esteemed one of the greatest proofs of a cook's skill."

Our own additions to these directions are first, to wash and wipe clean the tin reflector oven. Prepare turkey, using sausage dressing, and sew cavity closed.

Insert the spit all the way through the turkey and balance in the center. With strong string, tie wings and legs close to the bird, and also the tail. With more cord, tie the bird *very* securely to the spit so that there is no wiggle or wobble, using skewers if necessary to make firm.

Brush the bird liberally with melted butter. Place the bird in the oven in front of brightly burning hardwood coals, and keep coals coming in close to roaster for 3 or 4 hours until the bird is done.

Turn the spit frequently, and baste often with a combination of ½ cup melted butter, juice of 1 lemon, 2 Tbs. Worcestershire sauce in ½ cup of hot chicken or turkey broth. Salt and pepper the bird well after the last basting. The turkey is done when the drumstick is very soft, the bird is brown and glistening and tender. It is the best roast turkey in the world.

SAUSAGE AND SAGE DRESSING

For a large bird, in a heavy iron spider, brown 1 lb. spicy herb sausage (p. 36), separating it into crumbles as it cooks. Add 1 finely chopped onion, ½ cup finely diced celery. (If using storebought sausage, add 1 Tbs. sage, 1 Tbs. thyme, 1 Tbs. crushed rosemary, and mix in well.)

Pour the sausage mixture over at least 4 quarts of crumbled dry bread crumbs (no crusts, please) and mix well with fork and spoon. Add one or two cups of chicken or turkey broth (or water) and toss well until all the bread is moistened. The amount of broth used depends on your taste in dry or moist dressing.

GIBLET GRAVY

In a saucepan, cook the turkey neck, wingtips, and all the giblets except the liver in water to cover, adding a pinch of salt. Add a small peeled onion, several cloves, and a bay leaf. Simmer covered until the gizzard is tender, about 2 hours. Add the liver and cook another 15 minutes. Let cool in the water in which they were cooked.

When cool, remove giblets from broth and chop finely. Strain broth.

After the turkey has been taken from the fire, pour the drippings into a pan or jar. This fat may be used for cooking some other time. Scrape the brown crusty liquid at the bottom of the oven into a skillet. If necessary, add some fat to make about 4 Tbs. for each 2 cups of gravy wanted.

Heat the brown drippings and add 4 Tbs. flour (equal the amount of drippings), blend thoroughly, and cook and stir over low heat until well mixed and frothy.

Slowly add to the flour mixture two cups of giblet broth (thin cream may be added if there isn't enough broth). Stir constantly and blend well while cooking and thickening the gravy. Add the cooked and chopped giblets, from which tough membranes have been removed. Simmer for another few minutes until piping hot. Season with salt and freshly ground pepper to taste.

SPICED RED CRAB-APPLES

Choose only perfect red crab-apples. Wash, then cut out the blossom ends, but leave the stems on. Boil the apples in water to cover until tender but not mushy.

Boil together in a kettle 1½ quarts of good cider vinegar, 8 cups of light brown sugar, 2 sticks of cinnamon, and 2 tsp. cloves. Stir and boil until sugar is dissolved and the mixture becomes a thin syrup.

Pack the crab-apples in hot sterilized jars, cover them with hot syrup, and seal at once.

CREAMED ONIONS

Creamed onions is a traditional dish; no New England Thanksgiving table is properly set without it. Year after year, it is hardly touched at our house because there are so many other good things to eat. Even so, we wouldn't want to be without it on Thanksgiving.

Peel and cook in water to cover until tender but still firm about 2½ lbs. of small whole white onions.

In a large saucepan, melt 3 Tbs. butter, stir in 3 Tbs. flour, and add about 1½ cups thin cream (or half milk and half cream). Add ½ tsp. salt and a generous grind of pepper. Cook and stir until thick and creamy. Add the cooked onions, heat just to boiling again, and pour into a heated covered nappy. Grate a touch of nutmeg over the top.

MASHED POTATOES

Peel 1 large potato per person, and boil in salted water to cover until tender but not mushy. Drain well. With a wooden spoon, mash the potatoes until no lumps appear. Add 1 tsp. salt and a generous grinding of pepper. Add ½ to ⅔ cup of rich milk (for about eight potatoes) and a good lump of butter. Whip with energy until very fluffy and light. Pile into a hot dish; add another lump of butter to the top. Dust with paprika and a sprinkling of chopped parsley.

SQUASH SOUFFLÉ

Cut about 3 lbs. winter squash into pieces. Remove seeds and stringy bits. Cook in a kettle of boiling salted water until tender. Drain and cool.

When cool enough to handle, remove peeling from the pieces.

Place the meat of the squash in a kettle and mash well. Add and stir in 3 Tbs. melted butter, ⅓ cup brown sugar, ½ tsp. salt, a dash of cinnamon, nutmeg, and ground ginger. Add beaten yolk of 2 eggs and mix well. Fold in 2 Tbs. brandy and ½ cup chopped walnuts or pecans. Whip until stiff the whites of 2 eggs, and fold into the squash mixture. Pour into a buttered casserole or soufflé dish and bake in a moderate oven (350°) for 25 to 30 minutes. This does not puff up high, but it is a rich, light way of serving a favorite vegetable.

EBEN'S CRANBERRY SHERBET

Cook together until cranberries are tender and popped 1 lb. cranberries and 2 cups water. Put through a food mill or sieve.

Soften 1 Tbs. gelatine in ¼ cup cold water. Combine sieved cranberries with 1 cup water and 2 cups sugar. Heat just to boiling, then remove from fire and stir in softened gelatin. Cool.

When cooled, add juice and grated rind of 2 lemons and fold in the stiffly beaten white of an egg. Freeze in 2-quart freezer until firm. This is refreshing served with the turkey course in small glass cups.

OLD-FASHIONED CRANBERRY SAUCE

Boil together ½ cup sugar and 2 cups water until sugar is well dissolved, about 5 minutes. Add 4 cups cranberries and bring again to a boil. Do not stir, but boil over slow heat for another five minutes until all the skins have popped. Remove from fire and cool in the saucepan. Pour into jars and keep in a cool place until ready to serve.

CORNBREAD

There was cornbread at the first Thanksgiving in New England. In a simple form it was made by the Indians before us, as everyone knows. The Indians would be surprised at this light, delectable version of their staple.

If there is not enough left over for tomorrow's breakfast to eat with maple syrup, it takes only a few minutes to stir up another batch.

1 cup yellow corn meal	1 egg, slightly beaten
1 cup white flour	¼ cup melted, cooled butter
⅓ cup sugar	¾ cup milk
½ tsp. salt	3 generous Tbs. sour cream
4 tsp. baking powder	

Sift dry ingredients together in a yellow bowl, add milk, sour cream, beaten egg, and soft butter. Stir well with wooden spoon. Pour into greased iron corn-muffin pans (or into an 11-by-5-inch cake pan), and grate nutmeg over the top. Bake in a hot oven (425°) for 20 minutes, or until lightly browned on top. Serve and butter while hot.

PUMPKIN PIE

Have ready an unbaked 9-inch pastry shell with high crimped edges. In a bowl mix together thoroughly the following ingredients:

1½ cups cooked or canned pumpkin	3 eggs, slightly beaten
⅓ cup brown sugar	1½ cups rich milk
⅓ cup white sugar	½ cup heavy cream
½ tsp. salt	
1 tsp. ginger powder	
1 tsp. cinnamon	Have ready:
¼ tsp. grated nutmeg	1 cup heavy cream
¼ tsp. powdered cloves	1 Tbs. vanilla sugar (p. 12)

Pour first mixture into the prepared pie shell and bake in a hot oven (400°) for 50 to 60 minutes, until firm or until a knife-point inserted near the center comes out clean. Cool the pie well. Before serving, spoon over the top the heavy cream, which has been whipped very stiff and flavored with vanilla sugar.

MINCEMEAT

Mincemeat day is early in November. All hands help to peel the apples, chop the citron and the suet, and stir the ingredients. The receipt was handed down from ancestral kitchens in England, but a few innovations have been made through the succeeding generations. The final product may be stored for some time if kept in crocks in the cool butt'ry. Without the brandy it may be frozen or canned.

Cook until tender 3 lbs. of beef tongue or 3 lbs. of lean beef (top round). When cooked, remove any gristle or stringy bits.

Grind the cooked meat together with 2 lbs. of beef kidney suet (or very clear white beef suet). Put the meat–suet mixture in a huge bowl.

Add the following:

> 5 lbs. peeled, cored, and chopped apples
> 2½ lbs. seeded (not seedless) raisins (the seeded are puffier and
>   have a better flavor), separated (they tend to stick together)
> 1 pint sweetened seeded pie cherries
> 1 lb. shredded or finely chopped citron

1 Tbs. salt	1 Tbs. powdered cloves
2 Tbs. cinnamon	2 tsp. mace
1 Tbs. nutmeg	1 lb. sugar

> Melt 2 glasses of tart jelly (currant, beach plum, or choke-
> cherry) and stir into mincemeat

If the mincemeat is to be stored in covered crocks, add 1 quart (or a fifth) of good brandy and 1 bottle of good dry sherry. If it is to be canned or frozen, use instead 2 quarts of sweet cider. If cider is used, ¼ cup brandy may be added to the mincemeat when baking the pie.

MINCE PIE

In a bowl mix together:

2 cups mincemeat   ¼ cup brandy (if cider was used to
½ cup fresh chopped   make the mincemeat)
    peeled apple

Let stand while rolling out pie crust (p. 97). Put bottom crust into pie pan; spoon in mincemeat. If there are any dabs of jelly in the ice-box, melt and pour over mincemeat.

Put on top crust and flute edges together high and handsome. Bake in a hot oven (425°) until pie is well browned and piping hot. Serve with Brandy Hard Sauce.

BRANDY HARD SAUCE

Cream together 4 Tbs. softened butter, a pinch of salt, and 1 cup powdered sugar. Add 2 Tbs. good brandy; beat thoroughly until fluffy. Pass at the table in a cut-glass jelly dish.

CHAMPAGNE CIDER

Into a clean whiskey barrel pour fresh sweet cider made of clean perfect small apples; tangy Macs and Baldwins are good. Use 45 gallons of cider, then add 15 lbs. sugar and 5 lbs. honey (or 5 lbs. light brown sugar). Mix well. Add a little extra cider if necessary to fill the barrel. Cover the bunghole lightly with a wad of cheesecloth.

When fermenting ceases (one to three weeks), close the bung tightly. Some sediment will be in the bottom, so cider should be siphoned out from the top of the barrel. Cider may be bottled or left in the barrel. Serve well chilled.

ORANGE LIQUEUR

After a company dinner, in the prettiest of liqueur glasses serve your own orange liqueur, made in the winter when good oranges are plentiful.

Into a wide-mouth gallon jar put the rinds and juice of 6 or 8 washed oranges. Add the thin-sliced peel of 1 washed lemon. Add extra orange peel or tangerine peel for extra flavor.

Add 2 sticks of whole cinnamon and 1 tsp. coriander seed. Add 1 quart 100-proof vodka.

In a saucepan, boil together 2 cups sugar and 2 cups water until syrupy and reduced about half. (This may take about 45 minutes.) Cool the syrup and add it to the jar. Screw the lid of the jar on tightly, put jar in a large paper bag to keep the light out, and keep in a warm place in the kitchen or butt'ry.

Shake the jar each morning for five or six weeks. At the end of that time, filter the liquid through filter cloth until clear. Bottle the liqueur and let stand in dark cool place for at least six months before using. This receipt will make approximately 3 pints of delicious liqueur.

Thanksgiving day is nearly over. The dishes are stacked high in the kitchen waiting to be washed, but no one worries about them. Good family visiting goes on for a long time. All the old family stories are told, as they are every year, and there is much laughter mixed with some serious moments. The state of the nation is argued good-naturedly; the problems are all settled. The hearth-fire burns low, children are ready for bed, and there are all those dishes. . . .

Christmas

CHRISTMAS! This wondrous, exciting time is one each family celebrates with its own customs. Memories are sweet as we hold to ways of Christmases past.

Our own planning for this happy time begins with the day in January when the tree is taken down and the decorations are put away neatly in their attic boxes. "This string of lights is so worn we must get new ones"; "The squirrels have stolen nearly all the nuts from the front-door wreath— we'll have to make another." Nearly always "We didn't make enough cookies again. Double the double batches!" And "I liked best the truly handmade presents; let's always give things we've made ourselves!" All through the year we plan for Christmas.

Fruit-cake and plum-pudding days come in early November, for age and flavor. The batters are mixed with hands in the biggest bowls, and everyone in the family takes a turn at the mixing. Then they are packed

139

in pans to bake or steam and to be decorated with holly or balsam for Christmas presents, with plenty for our own butt'ry supply. Although we do this ahead of time in November, we aren't as foresighted as the keeper of a sixteenth-century inn in which we once stopped for lunch in England. Hanging on a rafter in the Great Room were nine rounded strange-looking objects which the innkeeper said were Christmas puddings. "We make them once every twenty-five years," he said. "We hang them on the rafters and use but one a year. When there is one left, we make another lot of twenty-five from a receipt that goes back to the founding of the inn." Our receipt goes back to our great-great-grandmother in England, but there is nothing in it to suggest that the puddings be aged as long as twenty-five years. (The receipt is here shared outside the family for the very first time.)

The real excitement begins to build up the day after Thanksgiving when presents are wrapped in Christmas paper and ribbon for mailing to faraway sister Eben and her family in Oregon, friends in Washington, Ginette in Paris, and cousins in England. When a tiny window or door on the Advent calendar is opened for the first peek and the Advent wreath with its red apples and candles is hung over the long table, the Christmas spirit is surging.

Whispered secrets are many. Presents are mysteriously hidden—sister Ruth declares dust ruffles were put on beds just for hiding things. Wreaths are made of fragrant balsam with two extra ones for the church doors, and ropes of ground pine and cedar are woven. Holly is cut and a kissing ball is made with mistletoe. Even the doll's house is readied, with its own tiny Christmas wreaths and tree and candles and presents.

Every day is full of preparation in the butt'ry. The goose hangs high. The fruit cakes are iced and then decorated with candied fruit. Batches of candy are made and packed in tins. Every available container for cookies is jammed to the brim, and the cooky-making days are the most fun of all. Make a dozen or more kinds and everyone has a hand in decorating with colored sugar, red peppermint candies, silver dragées, frosting in red and green, raisins and nuts. There will be lots of company all through Christmas-time and there must be a-plenty of everything good.

At last the boys are sent to the woods to find and cut the tree—always a tall one to touch the ceiling, symmetrical with full branches. It waits in the shed, its trunk in a bucket of wet sand, until decorating time. When it is brought in, no one but the "decorating committee" is allowed behind the closed parlor doors. From the attic come the ornaments, so many they crowd the tree, some of them so old they no longer shine except with sentiment. There are red and gold painted wooden hearts and horses and stars; angels with wax faces and real hair; silver balls and horns; and a real chipping-sparrow nest sprayed with gold containing three tiny eggs which once blew out of the rambler rose in a storm. Christmas-paper cornucopias are filled with candy and nuts; cranberry and popcorn strings drape the branches. Animal cookies and decorated eggshells and tiny gift boxes tied with gold ribbon and toy dishes and birds with spun-glass tails. On the top is the angel in a green velvet gown trimmed with lace of real gold and wings of gold too, holding high a tiny lighted star. All these and many more, each kept wrapped in tissue until time to hang in splendor on the Christmas tree.

The air is electric with excitement, and after the Christmas Eve service at the church it is hard to go to sleep, but suddenly it's Christmas morning. The stockings that were hung on the mantle are cramming-full of treats, an orange in the toe of each, hard candies, and gaily wrapped little packages of practical things: a box of pencils, thimbles for girls, knives for boys, a key ring for Father and a pincushion for Mother. (Do you remember the time Uncle Doug got only a sour lemon in his stocking because he had been very bad?) No one seems to find time or appetite for breakfast, but fruit and well-buttered slices of Great-Grandmother's Saffron Bread are on the sideboard and hold appetites until dinnertime.

Mother remembers that when she was small, after breakfast Grandfather would hitch the horses to the sleigh and the children and presents were loaded for a Merry Christmas ride to friends and neighbors. Now we fill the station wagon, making stops next door with a basket of cookies, then a wreath of balsam for the storekeeper, fruit cakes for neighbors, and a Merry Christmas for all.

Soon the company begins to arrive. The dinner table is set with its damask cloth ironed to shining smoothness and the big napkins to match. Tall red candles in silver candlesticks are paired on each side of a silver bowl of red apples and many-berried holly. The china and crystal and silver are set out and the prettiest dishes for jelly and relishes and candies.

A festive glass of Fountain Street Christmas Punch is passed to the grown-ups, plain cranberry punch for the children. Colorful as Christmas is the table's array of choicest of the year's butt'ry activity: pink applesauce, Waldorf salad flecked with red apple chunks, orange and red of the cranberry relish, sparking chokecherry jelly, snowy mashed potatoes, golden-dried creamed corn, and Hubbard squash. A first course of grapefruit and orange sections with red and green maraschinos is in place. By the time dinner is announced and the goose in all his glory is set on the table, eyes are popping and appetites are not wanting.

King Goose has been rich-fed for weeks to make him delectable and tender for today. Roasted on the spit in the tin oven, he has been pricked often as he roasted for self-basting and to allow the fat to be caught in the pan below. Nobody uses goosegrease for treating colds in our house any more, but we save it for cooking. The liver has been finely ground and combined with a bit of onion and thyme to make a most delicious pâté served in pastry shells with the punch before dinner. Now he comes to the table, crisp and brown and glorious on the platter, with a bed of parsley and surrounded by orange slices, red and green spicy apples, and small bunches of grapes. What a rich and splendid bird he is!

For dessert there is always our traditional flaming Old English plum pudding with brandy sauce—"Sauce Superbe" Sister calls it. When the pudding is lighted in the butt'ry, all lights in the Old Kitchen are extinguished except the candles on the table, and the flaming pudding is brought in, dramatic with a sprig of holly on top. For those who prefer, there is orange-lemon sherbet, an old favorite which is often on hand for our Very Special Occasions. Pass the mints and the candied orange peel and the jeweled cranberries. Take a cooky from the Christmas Cooky Tree. Enjoy a cup of family-favorite pot coffee, pass a tiny glass of homemade peach cordial to the grown-ups.

While the table is cleared and dishes are washed, contain if you can your excitement while Father reads Dickens' A *Christmas Carol* until Santa's sleighbells are heard ringing in the yard. How like Uncle Murray is Santa's voice—though no one suspects—as "Well, well, well, Merry Christmas, everybody" is shouted through the opening door. Then is the best parlor flung open, the tree with its golden sparkling lights and ornaments shown for the first time. Brought from the attic and underneath the tree are favorite toys of old—Grandmother's doll carriage, Father's first sled, Brother's first wagon jammed to the brim with bright-wrapped packages which spill over into the middle of the room. There is a deliciously long business of unwrapping packages one at a time as Santa passes them to outstretched hands when names are called. Oh the joy to a youngster in reading his own name on a handmade card, in admiring the ribbons and shining stickers and colorful wrappings, then the excitement in unwrapping and unfolding the present within! "It's just what I wanted"—over and over again.

At last Santa has gone, the boxes and papers and ribbons are put into baskets to be sorted tomorrow. Mother goes to the melodeon to play while we sing our favorite Christmas carols, with all the lights out except the Christmas tree and the twinkling star the green velvet angel holds. "It came upon a midnight clear, That glorious song of old. . . ."

Fruit Bowl

Saffron Bread and Butter

Coffee   Milk

SAFFRON BREAD

Great-Grandmother Thompson's receipt for Christmas Saffron Bread is simple: "Make a rich bread dough containing milk and eggs, enough for three loaves. Add saffron to the liquid about ½ teaspoonful a loaf. Knead in with the dough about three handsful of chopped candied fruit. Bake as usual. Cover with sugar icing."

More complete is Mother's adaptation for three loaves of delicious bread useful for Christmas giving and to have on hand for quick lunching on busy Christmas days.

Into a very large bowl put ½ cup butter, ½ cup sugar, and 1 Tbs. salt. Pour over this 2 cups scalded milk and stir until well mixed. When nearly cool add 2 cakes yeast and 1½ tsp. saffron soaked in 2 or 3 Tbs. warm (not hot) milk. Stir until dissolved and mixed.

Beat 3 eggs well, and add to yeast mixture.

Sift 7 cups flour with 1 tsp. mace. Stir flour into yeast mixture. Add ½ cup currants and 1 cup mixed chopped candied fruit. Mix with hands, adding a little more flour if necessary, until no longer sticky. Turn onto floured board and knead well for 10 minutes or so. Return to buttered bowl and cover with cloth. Let rise in warm place until double.

Cut dough into three parts; shape into loaves and place in greased 8-inch loaf pans. Brush tops with melted butter. Cover and let rise until loaves are puffy over top of the pan. Test by touching lightly with finger; if dent remains, loaves are ready to bake.

Bake about 40 minutes in hot oven (425°), placed well apart in the oven for circulation of heat, until loaves sound hollow when snapped with finger. They should be well browned. Remove from oven and cool on racks.

When cooled to just warm, pour over the loaves Sugar Icing made by stirring together 1 cup sifted powdered sugar and enough milk to make of a consistency to pour without being too thin. Add a little rosewater or a few drops of almond flavoring. Dribble nicely over the top of the loaves. May be decorated with sliced candied cherries or other fruits, although the bread looks attractive without the decorations.

CHRISTMAS DINNER

Fountain Street Christmas Punch   Iced Cranberry Punch (p. 92)

Goose-Liver Pâté in Tiny Pastry Shells

Grapefruit-Orange Sections with Maraschino Cherries

Roast Goose

garnished with Orange Slices, Spiced Red Apples, and Grapes

Red Applesauce   Waldorf Salad

Orange–Cranberry–Nut Relish

Chokecherry Jelly   Cloverleaf Rolls

Baked Hubbard Squash

Creamed Dried Corn   Mashed Potatoes (p. 133)

Old English Plum Pudding

with

Brandy Sauce Superbe

Orange-Lemon Sherbet

Candied Orange Peel   Mints   Christmas Cookies

Jeweled Cranberries

Coffee

Peach Cordial

FOUNTAIN STREET CHRISTMAS PUNCH

1 qt. cranberry juice (sweetened)

2 cups vodka

4 oz. Rose's lime juice (sweetened)

1 cup sparkling water

3 Tbs. sugar

Ice well; stir well; taste. This serves twelve people.

GOOSE-LIVER PÂTÉ IN TINY PASTRY SHELLS

Prepare half a receipt of rich pastry, and make tiny tart shells (p. 70). These can be made well ahead of time and kept in an airtight container.

Place the liver of the goose in salted water just to cover and bring to a boil. Cover the pan and simmer slowly for 20 minutes. Remove from fire and drain. Cut it into several pieces, then put through the fine blade of a meat grinder with 1 small peeled onion.

Make a paste of the liver and onion, adding 2 Tbs. of cooked chicken or goose fat or soft butter. Add ½ tsp. of freshly grated nutmeg, 2 Tbs. good cognac or brandy, a pinch of Colman's dry mustard, and ½ tsp. finely chopped thyme.

Mix thoroughly and pack firmly in a small bowl. Dust with finely chopped parsley and chill at least overnight. May be spooned into the tiny pastry tarts just before serving, or may be served with very small crackers.

GRAPEFRUIT-ORANGE SECTIONS
WITH MARASCHINO CHERRIES

With a very sharp knife peel grapefruit and oranges, cutting deeply so as to trim away the white layer of skin. Cut each side of each section down to the center, loosening the sections. Put sections into a bowl. Work over a bowl; the juice which drips as you work should be saved for adding to the servings.

Allow about four sections of each fruit for a serving, and alternate in a glass berry dish or champagne glass; pour the juice over, and for the grown-ups add a teaspoon of kirsch. On the top place sliced green and red Maraschino cherries arranged in a circle to simulate poinsettia flowers.

ROAST GOOSE

The *Buttery Book* called *Housekeepers Book by a Lady* is our valued reference for roasting a goose in the tin hearth oven, and the results are satisfying beyond any other method of roasting, as it was for the Thanksgiving turkey.

This delightful Lady recommends "Be careful in choosing a goose that the bill and feet are yellow, as it will then be young; when old, the feet and bill are red. When they are fresh, the feet are pliable; if stale, they are dry and stiff.

"The fire must be very quick and clear," she continues. "A goose should be stuffed with sage and onions, chopped small, and mixed with pepper and salt; boil the sage and onions in a little water before they are chopped, and mix bread crumbs with them when chopped to render them less strong.

"Put it first at a distance from the fire, and by degrees draw it nearer. Serve it with good gravy and apple sauce, in boats. It will take about an hour and a half to roast."

Our own method is to choose a fine goose weighing around 12 pounds, which will serve six to eight persons. If two geese are needed to serve the family, roast one in the oven of the kitchen stove and let the hearth-roasted bird be served first, when appetites can appreciate its superiority.

Remove all pin and other feathers and singe well. Rub the goose well inside and out with salt and pepper. Stuff with a bread dressing made of 2 cups bread crumbs and about 4 cups of chopped tart apples, 1 finely chopped onion, 1 Tbs. sage, salt, pepper, the whole moistened with ½ to ¾ cup rich milk. Truss the bird and tie well onto the roasting spit of the tin kitchen or hearth oven.

Prick the goose with a sharp-tined fork, particularly around the fatty areas of the legs and wings. As the goose roasts, keep the fire hot and watch the bird carefully, turning it often so it roasts evenly. Baste occasionally on top with fat drippings from the oven.

The process will take two to three hours, depending on the size, for a good bird to roast on the hearth, but judgment will have to be used. Do not let it get too well done or it will be dry. It takes a little longer to cook on the hearth than in the oven of a stove, as a rule.

The outside of the goose should be well browned and crisp. When done, remove from spit and place carefully on a large platter. Garnish with slices of orange, small bunches of grapes, and spiced crab-apples.

To make gravy, pour off the grease from the drippings in the bottom of the tin oven and use about 6 Tbs. brown bits and drippings. Put them in a saucepan or skillet over low heat. Add 5 Tbs. flour and blend and cook until smooth and bubbly. Slowly add 3 cups chicken stock or bouillon. Stir with a wire whisk and cook until thickened. Season to taste with salt, pepper, and a little powdered ginger.

RED APPLESAUCE

Pare, core, and cut into eighths eight fine firm flavorful apples. As they are prepared, drop them into a kettle of slightly salted cold water— just enough to cover. Bring to a boil in this water. If the apples are not tart, add the juice of a lemon. Add ½ cup sugar and about ⅔ cup red cinnamon candies. Stir gently with a wooden spoon, then simmer slowly until apples are tender. Serve in small glass dishes. This will make enough for up to twelve servings.

WALDORF SALAD

Wash 4 perfect red crisp apples. Cut into quarters and core but do not pare them. Dice the apples, leaving the red skins to add color. Mix the diced apples and ½ cup finely diced celery, ½ cup dates cut fine, and ½ cup diced pineapple. Dust with ½ tsp. salt and mix again.

Combine the fruit with enough mayonnaise to coat lightly, and mix with spoon. Pile into lettuce cups and surround generously with halves of pecans. Top with half a green Maraschino cherry. Makes up to twelve salads.

ORANGE–CRANBERRY–NUT RELISH

In a meat grinder with fine blade grind 1 pound raw cranberries and two large unpeeled quartered oranges from which the seeds have been removed. Add 2 cups of sugar to the fruit and ½ tsp. almond extract. Add 1 cup finely chopped (but not ground) pecan or walnut meats. Mix well. Chill thoroughly and pass at the table in a pretty bowl.

CHOKECHERRY JELLY

Gather chokecherries while firm and bright red, just ripening. Wash them, remove stems, and sort over carefully. Place them in a large kettle and add water just until it can be seen; do not completely cover cherries with it.

Bring to a boil and boil until cherries are soft and well cooked through. Force them through a coarse strainer, then put the juice into a clean jelly bag and let it hang overnight. Do not squeeze the bag.

Measure the juice and cook only four cups of juice at a time. For each four cups of juice measure out four cups of sugar, but do not combine them yet.

Place the four cups of juice in a large kettle (so the jelly will not boil over). Bring to a quick boil and boil rapidly for five minutes. Skim quickly, then add the four cups of sugar and stir in well until sugar is dissolved. Bring to a boil again and boil without stirring for five minutes.

With a large spoon, dip up a small amount of jelly, cool it, and let it drip slowly into the pan from the side of the spoon. When it reaches the sheeting stage (where two drops fall as one on the edge of the spoon—222° on a candy thermometer), the jelly is done and should be removed from the fire. Pour into sterilized jelly glasses and seal with paraffin. (Melt the paraffin, but if it is too hot it will shrink in cooling and cause the jelly to ooze.) Cover jars and store in a cool dark place in the butt'ry or cellar.

This is a tart, flavorful jelly that is perfect with game, fowl, and lamb.

CLOVERLEAF ROLLS

1 cup *hot* water	1 cup cold milk
½ cup sugar	2 eggs
1 tsp. salt	2 yeast cakes
½ cup butter	½ cup warm water
½ cup good lard	6 cups flour

Put sugar, salt, and shortening into hot water to melt; mix together well. Dissolve yeast cakes in warm water. Beat eggs and combine with milk.

Sift flour into large bowl; add all other ingredients and beat together until light and smooth. Cover with dampened clean dishtowel and put into ice-box several hours or overnight.

Two or three hours before baking, butter about two dozen muffin or gem cups. Form small pieces of dough into balls about an inch in size. Put three balls into each cup and brush with melted butter. Cover with dishtowel and let rise at room temperature until light. If rolls rise too fast, place in a somewhat cooler spot.

Bake in a hot oven (400°) until nicely browned.

BAKED HUBBARD SQUASH

Wash and cut in half a Hubbard squash. Remove seeds and stringy portions. Cut into neat 2-inch squares and place in a roasting pan that has a cover. Sprinkle the pieces with a touch of salt. On each piece put about a teaspoonful of butter. Add a teaspoonful of maple syrup and a small pinch of ginger to each piece.

Pour water to a depth of ¼ inch in the bottom of the pan; cover; bake in a moderate oven (350°) for an hour. Uncover, add more butter and maple syrup if necessary, and bake for another half hour, or until tender.

May be served on the platter around the goose or arranged on a plate and passed at the table.

CREAMED DRIED CORN

Corn-drying time is in August or early September, when the harvest is coming in and the hot dry days linger on.

Cook young tender corn in salted water for 10 minutes in a large kettle. Cut the corn off the cob and let the kernels drain.

Spread cooky pans with clean sheeting and spread the cut corn out thinly. Cover with a piece of coarse netting or cheesecloth and put outdoors in the sun. Stir occasionally.

When the sheeting is dry, remove it; then respread the corn on the bare cooky sheets and let it dry so thoroughly that it rattles when stirred. This may take several days (if so, bring the trays in at night).

When the corn becomes dry, put it in a cloth bag and hang in an airy place for several days to make sure there is no moisture left in the corn. Then put it in jars, screw on the caps, and store.

To cook the corn, soak 1 quart dried corn overnight in salted water to cover. Cook corn in this water until tender (about an hour) over low heat to simmer. When tender, drain the corn, season with 3 Tbs. butter, salt if needed, and pepper. Add ⅓ cup heavy cream; mix well, taste again for seasonings, and pour into a nappy. Up to twelve servings.

OLD ENGLISH PLUM PUDDING

1 lb. dry bread crumbs rolled
    fine (about 4 cups)
1 lb. flour (4 cups)
1 lb. sugar (2 cups)
1 tsp. salt
1 Tbs. cinnamon
2 nutmegs, grated
2 lbs. finely chopped suet

2 lbs. currants
2 lbs. seeded raisins
½ lb. mixed chopped candied
    peel
2 cups chopped peeled apples
12 eggs
Rind and juice of 2 lemons
¼ pint (½ cup) brandy
1 cup good sweet cider

Mix the dry ingredients well. Add the suet and fruits. Beat the eggs thoroughly and add the liquids, including lemon juice and rind. Add the eggs and liquids to the dry ingredients and mix together well.

Grease pudding molds well and fill molds about two-thirds full of mixture. Cover with parchment (buttered muslin or doubled heavy wax paper will do), tie it on, then steam in a covered kettle for three hours. Puddings improve with keeping. They may be reheated several times; reheating brings out the flavor.

This amount makes three large puddings; half the amount makes several small puddings.

To serve, reheat a pudding by steaming covered for about an hour. Turn onto a heatproof plate and place this plate on a silver tray. Decorate around the edge of the silver tray with sprigs of berried holly.

Heat 4 oz. (¼ cup) good brandy and pour over the pudding. At the kitchen door, light the pudding and bring it to the table flaming. Do not let the flame reach the holly, for it will burn. Serve with plenty of good brandy sauce.

BRANDY SAUCE SUPERBE

Cream 1 cup sugar and ⅓ cup soft butter. Add 2 whole beaten eggs (or 4 yolks) and 1 cup cream. Cook until slightly thickened, but do not boil. Add 1 tsp. vanilla and 4 Tbs. brandy. Serve in sauceboat and ladle over hot pudding.

This may be made well ahead of serving time and warmed over hot water at the last minute.

ORANGE-LEMON SHERBET

This receipt will make a gallon of sherbet.

6 oranges	7 cups rich milk
2 lemons	3 cups heavy cream
Grated rind of 2 oranges and 1 lemon	1 tsp. salt
3 cups sugar	1 Tbs. vanilla
	1 tsp. almond flavoring

Stir fruit juices and sugar together with grated rinds until sugar is well dissolved. Chill well. When ready to put into freezer, add flavorings, milk, cream, and salt. Freezing time is less when all ingredients are chilled to start.

CANDIED PEEL

Put orange (or grapefruit) peel which has been cut into dainty slices into cold water to cover and boil for 20 minutes. Drain and repeat five times, using a pinch of salt in the last water. The last time, boil until tender, then drain well.

Make a syrup of 2 cups sugar to 1 of water and boil until it spins a hair from a spoon. Add 1 Tbs. butter and the peel and let boil until the peel has absorbed all the syrup. Turn out on waxed paper that has been covered with dry sugar. Stir until well coated. Let stand a few hours to dry.

MINTS

In a bowl, beat together until well mixed:

White of 1 egg	3 or 4 drops wintergreen flavoring
3 Tbs. cream	Green food coloring

Add a little at a time, and mix well together, about 2½ cups sifted powdered sugar. When heavy enough to knead, use hands and knead well until very smooth. Shape into little balls about an inch in diameter and place on wax paper. Dip a fork into cold water, shake off excess water, and with the fork flatten the balls into round patties. Let stand until firm, then pack into boxes with waxed paper between layers.

Repeat this receipt, using red food coloring and peppermint flavoring.

Repeat, using vanilla flavoring without coloring.

Repeat, using lemon flavoring and yellow coloring.

This makes plenty of mints for serving at Christmas dinner and for garnishing the gift cooky and candy baskets.

JEWELED CRANBERRIES

Wash and dry a cupful of perfect cranberries, then prick each one four or five times with a darning needle.

In a saucepan, combine 1 cup sugar and 1 cup water and cook and stir until the sugar is dissolved. Then bring to a boil and cook without stirring until the syrup spins a thread about 6 inches long.

Add the cranberries to the syrup and cook until syrup reaches hard-ball stage in cold water (275°). Drain and dry the cranberries on a cooky sheet or wax paper. When nearly dry, roll them in granulated sugar and permit them to dry and harden thoroughly.

Put the jeweled cranberries into a silver dish. They are also a very pretty garnish for a cold-meat platter, served on little nests of parsley.

PEACH CORDIAL

Wash about five pounds of perfect ripe peaches, dry them, and cut them into quarters. Break half of the peach pits in two. Put the peaches and the broken pits into a gallon wide-mouth jar that has a tight-fitting screw lid.

Boil together two cups of sugar and two cups of water for about 45 minutes or until thick and syrupy. Cool this and add to the peaches. Add two sticks of cinnamon and 6 coriander seeds.

Over this pour a fifth or a quart of 100-proof vodka. Screw on the cover of the jar, put it into a large paper bag to keep it from the light, and keep it in the butt'ry or kitchen in a warm place for eight weeks. Occasionally stir the contents gently by holding the jar in your hands and swirling it a bit.

Filter the cordial until clear, then bottle. The peaches may be added to the tutti-frutti jar or may be cut into small pieces and served on ice cream for a dessert. This receipt will produce about three pints of cordial. It is best kept for six months before using.

For the Christmas Tree

Popcorn and Cranberry Ropes

Gilded Nuts

Crab-apples

Eggshells

Clove Apples

The Kissing Ball

Colored Popcorn Balls

Pies for the Birds' Tree

POPCORN AND CRANBERRY ROPES

Pop 1 cup of shelled popcorn. Pick over 1 pound of cranberries, saving only perfect berries. Thread a long, very thin needle with fine thread about a yard long. Tie an old shirt button to one end. Thread four or five popped grains of corn, then four or five inches of cranberries, alternating corn and berries until thread is nearly used up. Tie another button on the end.

Repeat this procedure many times, depending on the size of the Christmas tree. Plan to loop the strings between the branches, beginning at the top. Do not prepare the strings too far ahead of Christmas, for the cranberries, once pierced, will not keep well for too long a time.

GILDED NUTS

Crack large English walnuts by forcing a knife between the shells. Remove the meat and save for baking. Discard the thin inner shells. Glue the halves together, with a Christmas-cord loop at one end for hanging onto the tree. Holding the shells by this loop, dip each one into a small dish of gilt paint. Brush off excess. Hang on a curtain rod stretched between two chairs to dry. Or dip the shells into jars of high-gloss enamel in pretty colors.

Halves of the nuts may also be gilded or painted. Fill with tiny candies. Or trim and hang by gold cords to resemble a cradle or nest, with bits of moss, seeds, and dried plant materials.

CRAB-APPLES

At apple-harvest time, choose perfect crab-apples in various sizes and colors. Wash and polish and rub them with a little paste wax applied with a piece of toweling. Let dry, polish briskly, and set aside in a cool place to keep until tree-decorating time. Run a thin wire through the apple to hang on the tree.

These apples are beautiful for fruit and flower arrangements and for della Robbia wreaths.

EGGSHELLS

Choose fresh eggs and wash carefully, then dry. With a sharp needle, pierce the egg at both ends and run the needle in to break the yolk. Carefully enlarge the holes a little. Holding the egg with care, blow through one end until contents are emptied into a bowl. Rinse the shell in cold water and let dry. Thread gold or silver cord through the hole in the tip of the egg for hanging on the tree.

With sharp manicure scissors cut little doors in the eggs. Dip into Easter-egg dyes, or paint with oil or enamel colors. Trim the eggs with paper-lace trims, velvet or satin ribbons, jewels, sequins, and cordings. Fill the inside of the egg with other decorations, tiny scenes, flowers, or anything you've a mind to.

CLOVE APPLES (POMANDER BALLS)

Choose small perfectly formed apples and prick all over with a toothpick or blunt-end needle. Stick whole cloves into the apple so closely together that there is not room between for another clove. Make a loop with a small bow of red, green, or gold velvet ribbon and stick into the stem end of the apple with a small hairpin. Dust the apple with cinnamon and wrap it in tissue paper; set aside for several weeks to dry. The apple may be wrapped in colored net with a bow tied around the top for gift-giving. Very pretty and fragrant hung on the Christmas tree, in windows, or tucked into Christmas boxes for an old-fashioned touch of spiciness. After Christmas, hang them in the closets, tuck them into bureau drawers and chests.

THE KISSING BALL

From the butt'ry potato basket, choose a large, round, firm potato for each Kissing Ball to be made. Run a long thin wire through it carefully and loop the wire at each end back into the potato. This will give a loop at top and bottom for tying on the decorative ribbons.

Cut many short pieces of any of these Christmas greens: balsam, holly, boxwood, yew. The pieces should be about four inches long, clean and shining. Stick these pieces closely together into the potato, covering it entirely. A few shiny small red crabapples impaled on thin sharp sticks may be added for color if desired, neatly spaced among the greens. Tie a long red ribbon at the top of the ball for hanging. At the bottom, tie a generous piece of mistletoe dangled amid loops and ends of ribbon. This potato should keep indoors until Twelfth Night.

COLORED POPCORN BALLS

Pop about 10 cups of popcorn and put into a large dishpan.

Into a kettle put 1 cup white corn syrup and ½ cup granulated sugar and bring to a boil. Remove from the fire. Add one package of Jello—lime Jello for green popcorn balls, cherry or strawberry for red popcorn balls. Stir until Jello is dissolved, then pour over popcorn, mixing well with a wooden spoon. Butter hands lightly, then form the popcorn mixture into balls about the size of golf balls for the Christmas tree, or of tennis-ball

size for eating or other decorations. When thoroughly cool and dry, tie
with ribbon for hanging. If they are not to be used immediately, dry thoroughly, then store in large airtight can before tying on ribbons.

PIES FOR THE BIRDS' TREE

In a large kettle, melt two cups of leftover cooking fats (ham or bacon
grease is too salty for this). Add about two cups of peanut butter and mix
well. Remove from fire. Into the fats pour chopped peanuts, sunflower seeds,
raisins, and Grape-nuts to make a thick mixture. Pack into foil baking cups
or tuna-fish or other small cans. Trim with a sprig of holly or winter berries.
Hang with wire in a small evergreen tree out-of-doors.

For the Cooky Tree and the Butt'ry Cooky Jars

THE COOKY CHEST AND WHAT IT HOLDS

The cooky chest is an old pine chest with hand-wrought hardware and a mellow golden hue. Inside is a "safe," a box attached to the side that holds easy-to-reach cooky cutters. The chest is jammed full of equipment, and it slides under a shelf in the butt'ry so that it is always available. Here are some of the things it holds, and at Christmas everything is used:

Cooky cutters of all shapes and sizes
Watercolor brushes of various sizes
Toothpicks
Scissors
Bottles of food coloring (red, green, blue, yellow)
Red peppermint candies in little bottles
Colored sugars in little bottles
Silver dragées

Extra spatulas
Extra potholders
Extra measuring cups and spoons
The cooky press
Pastry tube for frostings
Paper leaves and stems for Marzipan
Gumdrops in various colors
Angelica
Small jars of cardamom and anise
Wooden sticks for caramel apples

In addition, we make sure there are other things at hand essential to the Christmas cooky making:

Plenty of cooky sheets—at least six
Cake-cooling racks—at least six
Flour sifters
Eggbeater
Wire whisks

Plenty of butter
Plenty of sugar
Plenty of flour
Plenty of eggs
Chocolate

Mixing bowls of various sizes

Custard cups for little dabs of colored frostings or sugars

Vanilla flavoring, almond flavoring

Lemon flavoring, peppermint flavoring

Pecans, walnuts, peanuts, butternuts, almonds

Dates

Raisins

Coconut

Candied fruits

Plenty of boxes and jars for packing away the cookies

Many spices always found on the butt'ry shelf

COOKIES TO MAKE AT CHRISTMAS

(In addition to receipts given on other pages in this book and listed in the index)

Brandy Cakes

Pfeffernusse

Spritz

Cutout Cookies

Mother's Orange-Almond Icebox Cookies

Holly Leaves

Honey Drops

Hazel's Jam Florentines

Liz's Chocolate Peppermint Sticks

Lemon Drops

Helen's Apricot Chews

Chocolate Coconut Chews

BRANDY CAKES

1 box (12-oz.) vanilla wafers (large-size box, about 75 wafers).

1½ lbs. pitted dates

4 cups shelled pecans

3 cups powdered sugar

⅔ cup brandy

Additional powdered sugar in a bowl

Crush the wafers finely with a rolling pin. Put dates and nuts through a food grinder. In a large bowl combine the wafers, dates, and nuts; add 3 cups powdered sugar and the brandy and mix well. The best way to do it is with the hands.

Using small amounts, about a teaspoonful at a time, roll the mixture into little firm bails about an inch in diameter, then flatten to make little cakes. Dip into a bowl of powdered sugar and coat well. Put on cooky sheet or waxed paper. When all the dough has been used, pack in a box with wax paper between layers.

The cakes will likely absorb the powdered sugar, so dust with additional sugar when serving the cakes or packing cooky boxes.

This receipt makes about 150 little cakes. They should be made a week before Christmas to be at their best flavor.

PFEFFERNUSSE

Many years ago, German neighbors kept us well supplied with pfeffernusse or peppernuts, which they always brought to us in a glass jar. They became one of the special Christmas flavors we found we couldn't do without, so we make them from an old German receipt.

4 eggs	2 tsp. cinnamon
½ cup softened butter	1 tsp. allspice
1½ cups brown sugar	1 tsp. mace
½ cup molasses	½ tsp. black pepper
¼ tsp. anise oil	1 tsp. ground cloves
6 cups flour	Grated rind of 1 lemon
1 Tbs. baking powder	1 cup finely ground blanched almonds
1 tsp. soda	½ cup chopped candied citron
½ tsp. salt	

In a large bowl beat eggs well; add butter, sugar, molasses, and anise oil. Sift together the flour and other dry ingredients. Add flour mixture to the egg mixture; add lemon rind and mix all together thoroughly. Add ground almonds and chopped citron and mix in well, using hands and kneading. Form dough into a ball; cover and chill for several hours.

Using part of the dough at a time, mold the dough into small balls about an inch in diameter. Place on greased cooky sheets, cover with wax paper, and leave overnight to dry a bit.

Bake in a moderate oven (325°) for about 15 minutes, or until nicely browned. Allow to cool on the pan a few minutes before removing to cooling racks. The cookies may be rolled in powdered sugar as they are taken from the pans or they may be frosted.

An easy way to frost them is to put a cup of powdered sugar into a shallow bowl and mix in enough brandy (or hot milk) to make a creamy mixture. When cookies have cooled, dip each one upside down quickly into the frosting, then allow frosting to harden before storing the cookies.

Store in airtight containers. If the cookies are not frosted, put a quarter of an apple into each container to keep cookies mellow and soft. There should be from 90 to 100 cookies.

SPRITZ

Spritz cookies are for the cooky press. Everyone loves to play with it, so make a great batch and press out tiny flowers, stars, twisted canes, holiday wreaths, and even small Yule logs with green frosting and chocolate-dipped ends.

2 cups soft butter	1 tsp. almond extract
1½ cups sugar	2 tsp. baking powder
2 eggs	¼ tsp. salt
1 Tbs. vanilla	5 cups flour

Cream butter and sugar together until light; add eggs and flavorings. Sift the flour with baking powder and salt, add to butter mixture, and mix thoroughly. Force through the cooky press onto ungreased cooky sheets (butter cookies do not require greased baking sheets).

Bake in a hot oven (400°) for 10 to 12 minutes. Do not brown these cookies; they should be a delicate golden color. This receipt will make about ten dozen various shaped cookies.

CUTOUT COOKIES

The *Buttery Book* receipt for cutouts is delicious to eat, firm enough for hanging on the Christmas tree, and excellent for decorating with piped or other frostings, painting with food color, and other decorating devices. We make it always in a double batch, which is just twice this receipt for about 75 cookies.

1 cup softened butter	1 tsp. almond flavoring
1½ cups sugar	4 cups sifted flour, resifted with
3 eggs	½ tsp. salt and 1 tsp. baking powder
1 Tbs. vanilla	

Beat the butter and sugar until light and fluffy. Add the eggs and flavorings. Add the flour mixture and beat or knead until smooth. Roll into two rolls, wrap in paper, and chill for several hours.

Using one roll at a time, roll dough out on a lightly floured board. If thin crisp cookies are wanted, roll the dough about $\frac{1}{16}$ inch thick; if soft, thicker cookies are wanted, roll about ⅛ inch thick.

The dough may be tinted lightly with food coloring to make green stars, pink hearts, or other fancies. Cookies may be sprinkled with colored sugar before they are baked, or they may have pieces of citron, nutmeats, raisins, dragées, or angelica pressed lightly into the tops.

Bake in a moderate oven (375°) until very delicately golden, usually 8 or 10 minutes. Watch carefully to make sure they are not overbrowned.

If the cookies are to be hung on the tree, before placing the baking sheet in the oven break off and work the large end of a toothpick carefully through the cooky and leave there during baking. When cookies are removed from oven, remove the toothpick end. When cookies are cool, a piece of ribbon or Christmas cord can be threaded through the hole.

When cool, some of the cookies may be frosted with a pastry tube.

PASTRY TUBE FROSTING FOR CHRISTMAS COOKIES

Beat until just frothy 3 egg whites. Add 1 lb *sifted* powdered sugar, ½ tsp. cream tartar, 1 tsp. vanilla. Beat until mixture holds its shape, adding more powdered sugar if necessary. Separate into small bowls or custard cups, mix in various food colorings, and force frosting through pastry tube, one color at a time. Keep a damp cloth or paper towel over the bowls to keep frosting from becoming dry. Add a drop or two of water to soften if necessary.

MOTHER'S ORANGE-ALMOND ICEBOX COOKIES

Cream 1 cup soft butter thoroughly and add gradually ½ cup sugar. Then add ½ cup brown sugar and cream well. Add 1 egg and beat well. Add 2 Tbs. orange juice. Sift together 2¼ cups flour, ½ tsp. salt, and ½ tsp. soda; add to first mixture, beating together well.

Add 1 Tbs. grated orange rind and ½ cup chopped blanched almonds rolled in ¼ cup flour. Mix dough well and with hands form into a roll, wrap in wax paper, and chill for at least 3 hours. The dough keeps well in the icebox for several days.

When ready to bake, cut in thin slices and bake on cooky sheets in a hot oven (400°) for about 8 minutes. Do not let them get too brown.

HOLLY LEAVES

These cookies are very pretty in the gift cooky baskets or on the cooky plates. Make one receipt of Cutout Cookies (p. 164), and tint the dough light green. If you do not have a holly-leaf cooky cutter, cut the leaf shape from a firm piece of cardboard, making it about 2½ inches long and 1½ inches wide. Then use a sharp-pointed knife dipped in flour for cutting around this shape.

Roll out the dough about ⅛ inch thick. Place cutouts on ungreased baking sheet. Two or three leaves can be pressed together at what would be the stem end of the leaves; some should be left as single leaves. Put one or two red cinnamon candies at the base of the leaves, and sprinkle the cookies liberally with green sugar. Bake as in directions for cutout cookies, being careful not to let the cookies get too brown.

Some of the leaves may also be outlined with green frosting after baking, with veins piped on; but we like them best with sparkling green sugar and the red cinnamon candies to simulate berries.

HONEY DROPS

¾ cup strained honey
½ cup sugar
2 well-beaten eggs
1 cup heavy sour cream
2 Tbs. melted butter
2½ cups flour

1 tsp. soda
1 tsp. baking powder
½ tsp. salt
2 tsp. vanilla
½ cup chopped candied citron

Mix all the ingredients together. Drop by small teaspoonfuls on greased cooky sheets an inch or two apart, as they spread. Bake in moderately hot oven (375°) until golden brown and firm.

167

HAZEL'S JAM FLORENTINES

2 cups sifted flour	½ cup raspberry jam
1 tsp. baking powder	⅔ cup chopped pecans
1 tsp. salt	
½ cup butter	*Meringue:*
1 cup sugar	2 egg whites
2 eggs	1 cup brown sugar
1 tsp. vanilla	1 tsp. vanilla

Cream butter, sugar, and eggs together. Sift dry ingredients together and add to first mixture, mixing well. Add vanilla. Spread in a well-buttered 8-by-13-inch pan.

Spread the first mixture with the jam, then sprinkle with the nuts.

Beat egg whites until frothy, slowly add the brown sugar and mix thoroughly. Add the vanilla. Spread over the mixture in the pan, and bake in a moderate oven (350°) for about 20 minutes, until nicely browned. Cool in the pan, then cut into squares and sprinkle with powdered sugar.

LIZ'S CHOCOLATE PEPPERMINT STICKS

1 cup softened butter	*Frosting:*
2 cups sugar	1 cup powdered sugar
4 beaten eggs	2 Tbs. soft butter.
1 Tbs. vanilla	1 Tbs. cream
4 squares melted chocolate	¼ tsp. peppermint flavoring
1 cup sifted flour	1 square melted unsweetened
1 cup finely chopped nuts	chocolate
	1 Tbs. butter

Cream butter and sugar together until light. Add eggs and vanilla and beat together well. Stir in melted chocolate, flour, and nuts and mix well.

Pour into two greased 8-inch square cake pans and bake in a moderate oven (350°) about 25 or 30 minutes. Cool thoroughly in the pan.

Mix powdered sugar, soft butter, cream, and peppermint flavoring together. When baked mixture is cool, spread with this frosting. Stir the melted chocolate and butter together until smooth, and dribble over the frosting. Chill until firm, then cut in bars about 2 inches by ¾ inch.

LEMON DROPS

Grate the peel of 1 lemon.

Cream 1 cup soft butter, add 2 cups light brown sugar and stir together until light and fluffy.

Add to this mixture and beat until smooth:

⅓ cup thick sour cream	Sift together:
2 eggs	3½ cups flour
1 tsp. vanilla	1 Tbs. ground ginger
1 tsp. lemon extract	2 tsp. soda
Grated rind of the lemon	2 tsp. cream tartar
	1 tsp. salt

Stir flour mixture into first mixture and mix together well. With a teaspoon, dip out small amounts of dough and roll in the hands into small balls, less than an inch in diameter. Place about 1½ inches apart on buttered cooky sheets. Bake in a slow oven (325°) about 15 minutes or until lightly brown.

Remove carefully from pan at once, and dip each cooky into a mixture of ½ cup light brown or white granulated sugar and 1½ tsp. cinnamon (grated lemon rind may be used instead of cinnamon). Shake off excess and cool on wire cake racks. This makes about 75 cookies.

And two confections that children like to make:

HELEN'S APRICOT CHEWS

Put one box of dried apricots through the meat grinder. To the ground apricots, add 1 box (about 2½ to 3 cups) of flaked or shredded coconut and 1 15-oz. can of sweetened condensed milk. Mix all ingredients well. Drop by half-teaspoonfuls on well-buttered cooky sheets. Bake in moderately hot oven (375°) for 10 to 12 minutes, until cookies are slightly toasted on top and lightly browned on the bottom. Remove at once from cooky sheet and cool on cake racks. About 75 cookies.

CHOCOLATE COCONUT CHEWS

In the top of a double boiler, melt 2 squares unsweetened chocolate. Add one 15-oz. can of sweetened condensed milk, 2½ to 3 cups shredded coconut, ½ tsp. salt, and 1 tsp. vanilla. Mix all together thoroughly.

With two teaspoons, or one teaspoon and deft fingers, make little rounded dabs of the mixture and place on well-greased cooky sheets. Do not make the drops too large—about a half-teaspoonful makes prettier cookies.

Bake in moderately hot oven (375°) for 15 minutes. Remove from cooky sheet immediately and cool on cake racks. Store in a covered tin. About 75 cookies.

For the Candy Jars

Mason Girls' Old-fashioned Fudge

First Lady's Fudge

Sis's Penuche

English Rum Toffee

Maple Caramels

Eben's Divinity

Fondant for Stuffed Dates

Marzipan

MASON GIRLS' OLD-FASHIONED FUDGE

In a large saucepan over low heat, melt 4 squares unsweetened chocolate. Add and stir in quickly 4 cups sugar, 1 cup milk, a pinch of salt, ½ cup heavy sweet or sour cream, and 2 Tbs. light corn syrup. Stir together and cook over low heat until sugar is dissolved and candy comes to a boil. Continue to cook without stirring until the candy reaches soft-ball stage (when a little dropped into a cup of cold water makes a soft ball; 238° on the candy thermometer). Do not let fire get hot enough to burn candy.

Remove from the fire and add 2 Tbs. butter. Cool the candy until just warm to the touch, then beat in the butter and continue to beat until the fudge becomes thick. Add 1 Tbs. vanilla and ½ cup chopped butternuts (or black or English walnuts). Drop by teaspoonfuls on wax paper or cold buttered cooky sheets and let harden. Or pour into a buttered platter, and when cool cut in squares.

FIRST LADY'S FUDGE

This is a modern receipt made famous by a gracious First Lady, which we thought was so delicious we copied it into *The Buttery Book*.

In a large bowl, put 2 cups (12 oz.) of semisweet chocolate bits; 3 bars (12 oz. total) of chopped German sweet chocolate; 1 pint (2 jars) marshmallow cream.

In a saucepan, put 4½ cups sugar, a pinch of salt, 2 Tbs. butter, and 1 tall can of evaporated milk (1⅔ cups).

Bring this mixture to boil, stirring; then reduce the fire and simmer gently for 6 minutes.

Gradually pour the boiling syrup over the chocolate mixture in the bowl, and beat well until chocolate is melted and ingredients are well mixed. Stir in 2 cups chopped nuts.

Pour into buttered pan and cool for a few hours, until hard enough to cut into squares.

SIS'S PENUCHE

In a heavy saucepan over low heat, melt 2 Tbs. butter. Add 1 cup white sugar and 1½ cups brown sugar and a pinch of salt. Add gradually and stir well ½ cup whole milk and ½ cup heavy cream mixed together. Keep heat low and continue to stir until sugar is completely dissolved, using a wooden spoon.

When mixture boils, let boil slowly to soft-ball stage (238° on the candy thermometer). Remove from fire and let stand without stirring until cool. Then beat until thick and creamy.

When cool, add 2 tsp. vanilla and ½ cup chopped butternuts (or black walnuts). The candy may be dropped with teaspoons onto wax paper or poured onto a buttered platter, then cut in squares.

ENGLISH RUM TOFFEE

1 cup cream	½ cup butter
1¾ cups sugar	2 tsp. rum
Pinch of cream of tartar (⅛ tsp.)	

Put the cream, sugar, and cream of tartar into a large saucepan over a rather hot fire, mix well, and stir until they come to a boil. Continue stirring and boil the ingredients, add the butter, and bring to the small-crack stage (English term for what we call the "hard-ball stage," when the candy dropped into a cup of cold water forms a firm ball—290° on the candy thermometer).

Remove from heat, quickly stir in the rum and pour into a well-buttered pan. While cooling, cut into small squares. When quite cold, break off the pieces, wrap in foil.

MAPLE CARAMELS

2 cups brown sugar	Pinch of salt
1½ cups maple syrup	1 Tbs. butter
½ cup cream	½ cup chopped butternuts (or black walnuts)

In a large saucepan, combine the sugar, maple syrup, and cream; stir and bring to a boil. Boil slowly until candy reaches the soft-ball stage (250° on the candy thermometer). Remove from the fire, add the salt, stir in the butter and butternuts. Pour into a well-buttered pan. When cold, cut into squares. Let harden, and when quite firm, wrap in wax paper or foil.

EBEN'S DIVINITY

2 cups sugar
½ cup water
½ cup light corn syrup
2 egg whites

1 tsp. vanilla
½ tsp. almond flavoring
1 cup chopped nuts

Stir the sugar, water, and corn syrup together over low flame until sugar is dissolved. Bring to a boil, then boil covered without stirring until it stands stiff like spun glass when tried in cold water (250° on the candy thermometer).

Beat the egg whites until stiff. Pour the hot syrup over the egg whites and beat until the mixture begins to lose its glossiness. Add flavorings and nuts. Drop by teaspoonsful on a platter to cool; or pour it all at once into a 7-by-11-inch buttered pan and cut into squares when cool.

FONDANT FOR STUFFED DATES

2 egg whites
4 cups sifted powdered sugar

4 tsp. soft butter
1 tsp. vanilla
½ tsp. almond flavoring

Combine all the ingredients and mix well, kneading with hands. Remove the pits from dates, fill with fondant, reshape dates neatly. Dip into powdered or granulated sugar.

MARZIPAN

This traditional confection is so fascinating to play with that it should be made several weeks before Christmas, well before the last-minute rush. Then it can be stored in airtight tins; it keeps well. We once made marzipan strawberries for a winter tea party and had such fun doing it that we forgot the sandwiches.

Marzipan can be made from boughten almond paste, which is very expensive. Or it can be made rather laboriously from almonds at a much smaller cost. Make the paste a week before making the candies, as it needs time to ripen properly.

Blanch a pound of shelled almonds by dropping them into boiling water, then slipping off the skins. Our *Buttery Book* directions say to "pound them in a mortar," but we suggest putting them through a food grinder with the finest blade. Grind them three times.

In a saucepan, cook 2 cups sugar and 1 cup water until it reaches the fine thread stage (when the syrup dropped from a spoon spins a fine thread at least 6 inches long; 240° on the candy thermometer). Remove from the fire.

To the syrup add the ground almonds and about 6 Tbs. orange flower water (drug store). Stir, then knead until well blended. If too stiff, add water a drop at a time and work in carefully. Pat out on a large platter or marble slab and leave until thoroughly cooled. Pack into a bowl and cover securely for a week.

To make the marzipan fruits and flowers, beat 1 egg white until frothy. Work in a handful (about a cup) of almond paste, then add powdered sugar to thicken until it is no longer sticky. Knead well until it is smooth and thick enough to mold and hold its shape firmly. Keep covered with damp cloth while working on each separate piece of candy.

Gather together custard cups, paint brushes, liquid or paste food coloring, colored sugars. From Dennison's in New York there can be bought paper stems and leaves for fruits and berries, but they can also be made at home from colored paper and toothpicks or wrapped wires. Dilute food colorings in water, each color in a separate custard cup.

Mold the candies into the desired shapes, tint with coloring. For potatoes, make eyes by denting the shaped potato with a small nailhead, then roll in cocoa. For strawberries, shape, color, brush on a little water and touch with red sugar. Pebble the surface of oranges and lemons by touching lightly with a fine grater. Try your hand at peas in the pod, bananas, carrots, pears, peaches, and apples. Dust the peaches with powdered sugar, very lightly, to make fuzz. It helps to have real fruits and vegetables on hand for models if imagination lags.

Wrap or store each piece as it is made to keep from drying. Pack in prettiest baskets and containers lined with lace-paper doilies, and wrap carefully and gaily for gifts.

The Fruit Cakes

FRUIT cakes should be made well before Christmas, even as early as mid-November. They are best when sprinkled with brandy and wrapped snugly in foil, then kept for a month or six weeks before being used. We do make an exception in the case of Miss Ida's Rich Plum Cake, which we make a week before Christmas.

It takes a special trip to town to gather all the materials. It takes one or even two days of devotion to the making, and everyone takes a turn at the stirring of the heavy mixtures—even visitors who choose that day to pay a call. The pans are well buttered, the fruit is prepared, the oven is ready.

Miss Ida's Rich Plum Cake (p. 21)
Fruit Cakes for Christmas Baskets
Aunt Frannie's Fruit Cake

FRUIT CAKES FOR CHRISTMAS BASKETS

Mix together to make 2 quarts (about 3½ lbs.) diced candied fruits and peels including:

Candied orange peel   Candied pineapple
Candied citron   Candied red and green cherries
Candied lemon peel

Add: 2 cups diced dates   4 cups flaked or shredded
2 cups blanched chopped almonds   coconut
1 cup white seeded raisins   1 cup diced dried apricots

Sift together: 1 Tbs. baking powder   1 Tbs. salt
4 cups flour

Pour 1 cup of the flour mixture over the prepared fruit, and mix well to coat.

In a very large bowl, cream together:
2 cups soft butter   ½ cup brandy
2 cups sugar

Add, one at a time, and beat well after each addition:
10 eggs

Add flour mixture to the butter mixture, then add slowly 1 cup pine-apple juice or sweet cider, beating well until thoroughly blended. This is best done with a sturdy long-handled wooden spoon. Add the fruit mixture and stir thoroughly, using hands if necessary (the mixture becomes hard to handle with the spoon).

When batter is well mixed, spoon it into liberally buttered tiny bread or cake pans. Place well apart on oven shelves to allow good circulation of heat and bake in slow oven (250°) for about two hours, until browned on top and firm.

This receipt will make about 10 small cakes. They may be left in their baking pans for gifts, or they may be cooled on cake racks, then sprinkled with brandy and wrapped securely in foil, tied with Christmas ribbons and a sprig of balsam. If desired, they may be iced and decorated with candied fruit or nuts.

ICING FOR FRUIT CAKES

Mix together 2 cups powdered sugar and just enough boiling water to moisten. Stir until smooth; add ½ tsp. lemon extract. Now add a little more boiling water, until icing is just of the right consistency to pour thickly. Pour over tops of cakes only. Let cool a moment, then add candied decorations. Let frosting harden completely before wrapping for gifts.

AUNT FRANNIE'S FRUIT CAKE

Aunt Frannie sends her fruit cake to us through the mails each Christmas well packed in a sturdy tin box. It is so delectable that we begged for the receipt to enrich *The Buttery Book*. "Why, bless your heart, I'm proud for you to have it," replied this gracious North Carolina lady.

1 lb. red candied cherries
1 lb. green candied cherries
2 lbs. candied pineapple
2 lbs. white raisins
½ lb. candied lemon peel (ground)
½ lb. candied citron (ground)
½ lb candied orange peel (ground)
½ lb. Brazil nuts (coarsely chopped)
1 lb. blanched almonds (halved)

4 oz. flaked coconut
1 dozen eggs
1 lb. butter
1 lb. sugar (2 cups)
1 lb. flour (4 cups)
1 oz. lemon extract
1 cup brandy or bourbon whiskey
1 bottle white port wine

Soak fruit and nuts overnight in all of the wine minus one cup. Save the cup of wine for later.

Have oven at slow heat (250°). Separate eggs and beat yolks and whites separately. Cream sugar and butter well. Add beaten yolks and flour alternately, and beat well. Gradually add lemon extract and 1 cup white port wine. Beat well. Fold in beaten egg whites.

Pour this mixture over the wine-soaked nuts and fruit. Mix with hands and add 1 cup brandy (or bourbon whiskey) and mix a little more.

Bake for 3 or 4 hours. Use 3 large greased paper-lined tube pans. When cakes are done, wrap entire pans in foil and cover with big bath towels until completely cool, overnight at least. Then remove cakes from pans and store in airtight containers.

Many, many years ago there was a charming year-end custom in Old Hampshire, England. Children went from house to house carrying a wooden wassail cup, trimmed with ribbons and a golden apple at the top, begging for pennies and singing these words:

Wassail, wassail, to out town;
The cup is white and the ale is brown;
The cup is made of the ashen tree,
And so is the ale of the good barley.
Little maid, little maid, turn the pin,
Open the door and let us in;
God be here, God be there,
We wish you all a Happy New Year.

Glossary

Bouquet garni—a bunch of herbs tied together for cooking; used in soups, stews, and gravies. Could be a combination such as thyme, parsley, celery or lovage leaves, cloves. Often the combination is tied in cheesecloth; remove before serving.

Clove apples (now called *pomander balls*)—apples with cloves stuck in closely; used for scenting closets, linen chests, and the like.

Cornucopia—A cone of paper or cloth with a small opening at base from which is squeezed ornamental frosting for cakes and cookies. Also, a cone made of decorative papers, filled with candy, cookies, or flowers, with a handle for hanging on doorknobs (May Basket Day) or Christmas tree.

Dash—1/16 tsp., usually of salt or spice.

Dipsy Do's—chocolate-coated goodies.

Foil—a modern invention that Grandmother would have loved for her kitchen, particularly for wrapping hearth-baked (but not oven-baked) potatoes instead of mud.

Gem—originally a muffin made of coarse or unleavened flour: we use the term loosely for *muffin*.

Gem pans—cast-iron cooking pans for gems or muffins.

Granite, graniteware—enamelware.

Lovage—a leafy herb with a strong taste of celery.

Mac—New England's favorite crisp red apple, the MacIntosh.

Mortar—a wooden, iron, or pottery vessel in which grains, herbs, or other substances were hand-ground with a club-shaped instrument called a *pestle*.

Muster field—a village field used since the Revolution for training and drilling local militia.

Nappy—a round or oval dish with a flat bottom used as a baking or serving dish.

Pestle—a clublike instrument used for grinding herbs, grains, and the like in a mortar.

Pinch—about ⅛ tsp., according to taste; usually of salt or spice.

Receipt—recipe, or rule for cooking.

Rule—dialectic term for receipt or recipe.

Skillet—a small metal cooking vessel with feet; a *spider*; a frying pan.

Spider—a cast-iron pan with a handle, used for frying. Originally with legs, it was used over coals on the hearth.

Spurtle—a Scottish kitchen instrument; a wooden stick for stirring porridge and the like.

Thimble—1 teaspoonful.

Tin kitchen—a tin reflector oven with a spit; used in roasting meats on the hearth.

Turk's head mold—a tube cake or pudding mold with a swirled design.

Wassail—a toast of ancient Saxon origin meaning "To your health."

Index

Sherbet:
  cranberry, Eben's, 134
  orange-lemon, 153
Shortbread, Scotch, 118–119
Shortcake, 88
Sirloin steak, 102–103
Sis's penuche, 171
Songs:
  for baking cookies, 46
  wassail, 179
Soufflé:
  Grand Marnier, 77–78
  squash, 133–134
Soup:
  hot tomato, 101–102
  jellied chicken consommé, 39
Spiced cider, 20
Spiced red crab-apples, 132–133
Spiced tea, 56
Sponge cake, lemon, 42–43
Spring tea party, 53–56
Spritz cookies, 163–164
Squash, baked Hubbard, 151
Squash soufflé, 133–134
Steak:
  filet mignon (tenderloin), 75
  sirloin, 102–103
Stuffed dates, 173
Stuffed eggs, 82
Stuffing: See Dressing
Sugar, vanilla, 12
Sugar cookies, Mother's, 29–30

Taffy for pulling, 123
Tarts:
  jam, 70
  pumpkin, 124–125
Tea:
  iced, 96

minted iced, 57
  spiced, 56
Tea parties:
  afternoon, 53–63
  garden (summer), 56–60
  spring, 53–56
  thimble, 116–119
  winter, 60–63
Tenderloin, beef, 75
Thanksgiving, 127–138
Thimble tea, 115–119
Thimble tea chicken salad, 116–117
Toffee, English rum, 172
Tomato soup, hot, 101–102
Tomatoes, fresh, with cucumbers, 103
Turkey, hearth-roasted, 130–131
Tutti-frutti sauce, 10–11
Twelfth Night cake, 20–21
Twists, orange, 41–42

Valentine's Day, 27–31
Valentine's Day cake, 30–31
Vanilla, 12
Vanilla custard ice cream, 83
Vanilla ice cream, country, 43
Vanilla sugar, 12
Vegetables:
  asparagus spears, 76
  corn pudding, 40
  corn, creamed dried, 151–152
  green salad, 77
  onions, creamed, 133
  peas, new, 93–94
  potato salad, 81–82
  potatoes au gratin, 40–41
  potatoes baked on the hearth, 75
  potatoes, mashed, 133
  potatoes, parsleyed new, 93
  squash, baked Hubbard, 151

squash soufflé, 133–134
  tomatoes with cucumbers, 103
Violets, candied, 24–25

Waldorf salad, 149
Walnut brittle, Hattie Hoyt's, 123
Wassail song, 179
Watercress sandwiches, 58
  rolled, 67
Watermelon, melon bowl, 93

Wedding anniversary dinner for two, 73–
  78
Wedding cake:
  bride's, 71–72
  groom's, 71–72
  icing, 72
Wedding reception, 65–72
Whole-wheat bread, 82–83
Winter tea party, 60–63

Yorkshire pudding, 113